# Modest Gifts

TO NORRIS

# Modest Gifts

POEMS AND DRAWINGS

Norman Mailer

RANDOM HOUSE TRADE PAPERBACKS NEW YORK

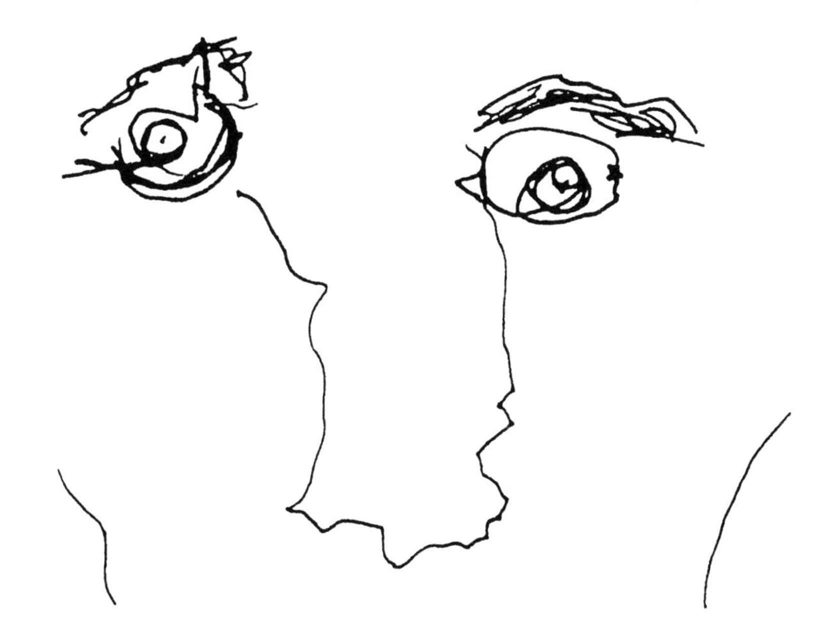

I don't know
where to
start

Well, in fact I do know. It is to warn the buyer. For the title is accurate—the gifts you will purchase are modest. William Merrill once wrote that a poem which was too easy to read was without value. "Difficult surfaces [can work] through to the poem's emotional core."

These pieces, for the most part, will be comprehensible on first approach. Some barely qualify as poems. They are snippets of prose called short hairs, there to shift your mood a hair's width. Perhaps one element of a good poem is its power to succeed in altering a reader's mood, but I will make no such claim for most of these inclusions, and something of the same can be said of the drawings. Is one to call them caricatures, cartoons, squibbles, or doodles? At best, they are line drawings—shading is beyond my means. If I now combine these line drawings with the short hairs, it is to offer the reader an easy pleasure. My serious work, such as it is, does not always accomplish this. Nor does it always want to. I belong to that dwindling group of novelists who wish to make a demand on their audience. I want the reader to owe a little more to the work than some passing gratitude for the mild enlivening of his or her leisure time. My mind was shaped at an early age, after all, by the great Russian novelists with their implicit expectation that you, the reader, are there to suffer with the writer. Why? For a huge reason—to partake of the ongoing quest to deepen our comprehension of life and eternity, as if—for fact!—life and eternity cannot survive without such a quest.

I still believe this. But by the age of eighty, tolerance insists on seeping into dedication. Casual pleasures become more meaningful even as lively pleasures sleep, and a

few pains turn chronic. So, amusement becomes more of a virtue in itself. I now like to think that a limited ability to draw when coupled with a merry pretension to write poetry can turn sometimes into more than the sum of its parts, even as a minus times a minus will produce a plus. In mathematics, that always operates. In art, it can happen now and again. Obviously, I hope this is such an occasion.

I am not, however, being altogether candid. There are a few good poems and a few good drawings here. Which ones they may be, I keep to myself. My real pleasure will come if twenty different candidates are nominated by a score of men and women.

Here, I must offer a further confession. I knew this unashamedly self-serving attitude would have to disclose itself—modesty (at least for me) is too harsh a stricture to maintain all the way through two pages of a preface.

One more note:

A few poems were revised for this edition, but most were written in the early Sixties and published in a book called *Deaths for the Ladies (and other disasters).* The rest appeared by 1965 in *Cannibals and Christians.* Most of the drawings were done, however, in recent years. Nonetheless, the sketches are not all that removed from the tone of the short hairs, even if my ongoing mood in those years when the poems were written was considerably more intense. So I think it's appropriate to include an appendix in this book. It is the introduction I wrote for a mass-market paperback edition of *Deaths for the Ladies,* which came out almost ten years after the first publication in 1962, and it will offer a subtext to those readers who find themselves somewhat intrigued by what follows.

# I

# Cocktail Party

## A. Voices

Don't speak to me until I've had a drink.

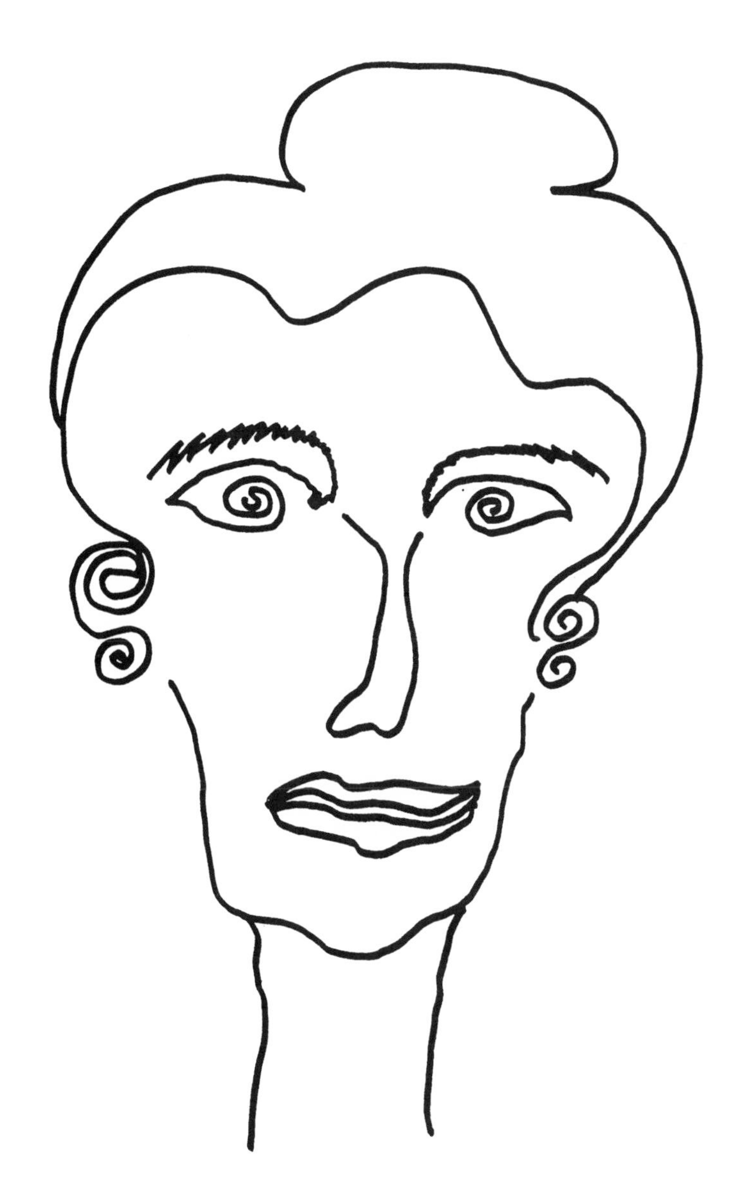

I never dreamed that I would be the one to sell our family home.

My mother tells me
that I would be a
beauty if I would
just pull myself
together.

options.com shoot me
an E-mail.

Sometimes I feel
as if I have a
picture of the whole.

Sometimes I feel
as if I have no grasp
of it at all.

I
was
hysterical
stated
the girl

            I
dropped
my
   god
damned con
tact lens
   down
   the drain

Then
this
creep
called at four
           A.M.

Hel
    lo Kook
    he said

Guess what:

    I just
    found
    your
    contact
    lens.

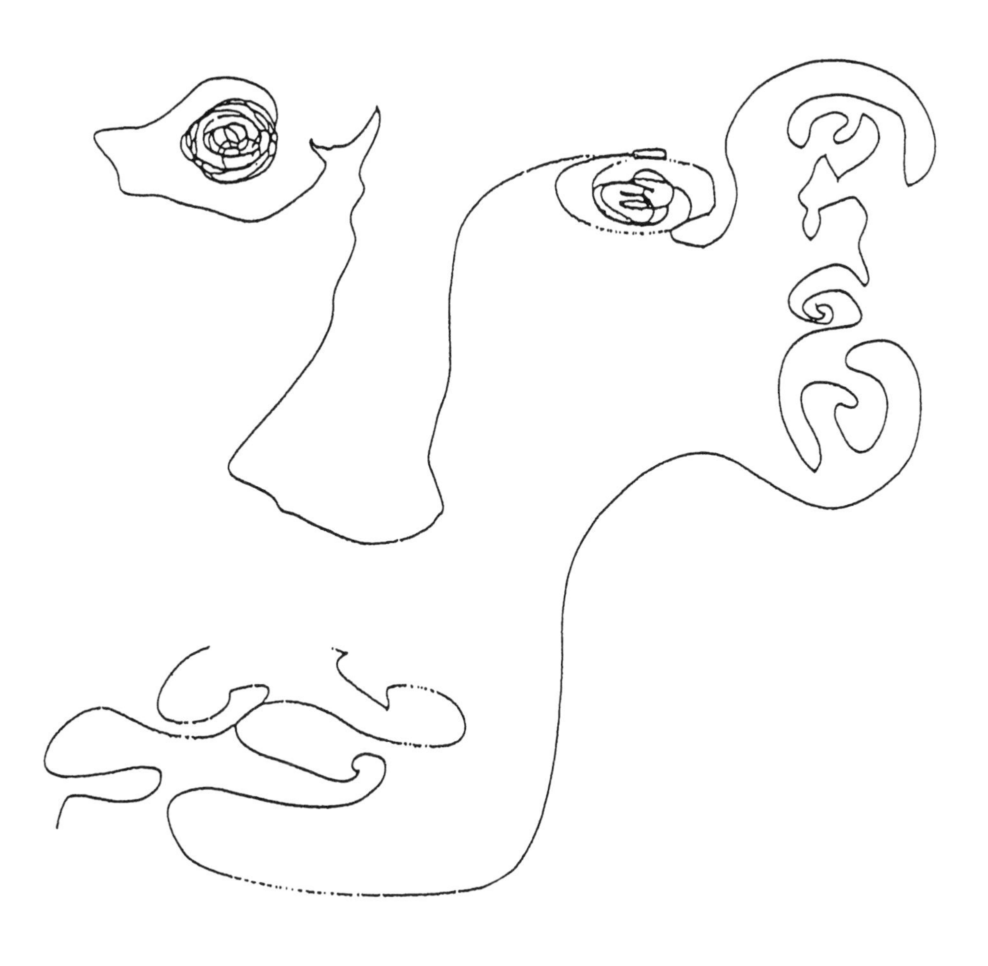

I feel
as if
I'm begining
to look like
my cell phone.

My new date is fantastic. Don't try to steal him.

Don't try to tell me, Randy, that Pablo P. didn't know what it was all about.

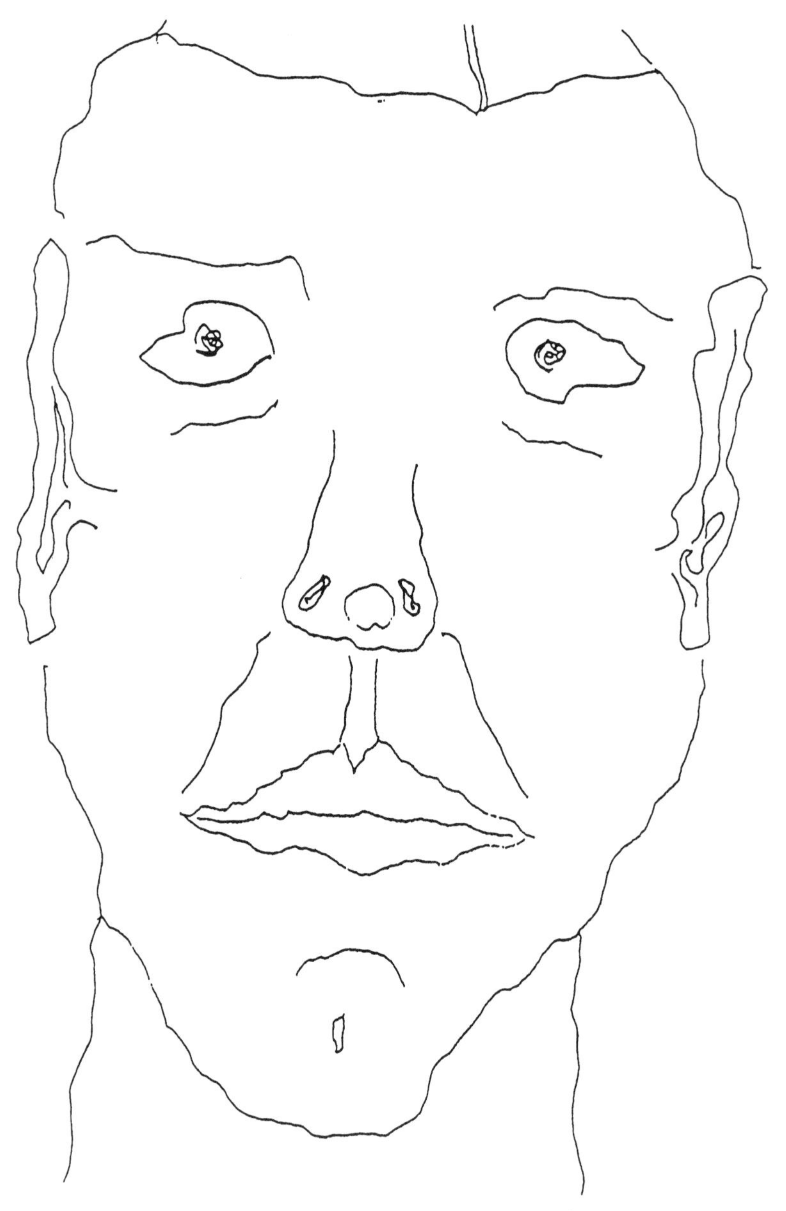

I don't really believe
that I am gay. It's just . . .

How can you
     say
you're
  only
  three-quarters
          a man,
why you're
        completely
        a man
        said the
            lady
            in a
            three-quarter voice.

I still
love
him
deeply
    she said
    deeply
    out of her
    double
    chin.

I must say I am
not happy being
a divorced man.

I've made money
all my life. So,
why do I feel
punched-out?

The
cigarette
smoker
said

I'd
rather
waste it
than give
it

away

America should have
two churches
one for people
who smoke
and one for those
who don't

I think
I'll switch
from ginger ale
    now

to a
nice
    glass
    of
    soda.

Drinker
with a
problem said:
I'll drink
to that.

I'm getting
very little
out of this.

I'm getting nothing

Can't you see?
It's time to leave.

# Cocktail Party

## B. Lingerers, Laggards & Blackguards

Why can't Garry Trudeau find a spot for me?

This much
I know.
Speed will
never
betray me.

Just let me kiss
her once and she
will kiss me back
a hundred times

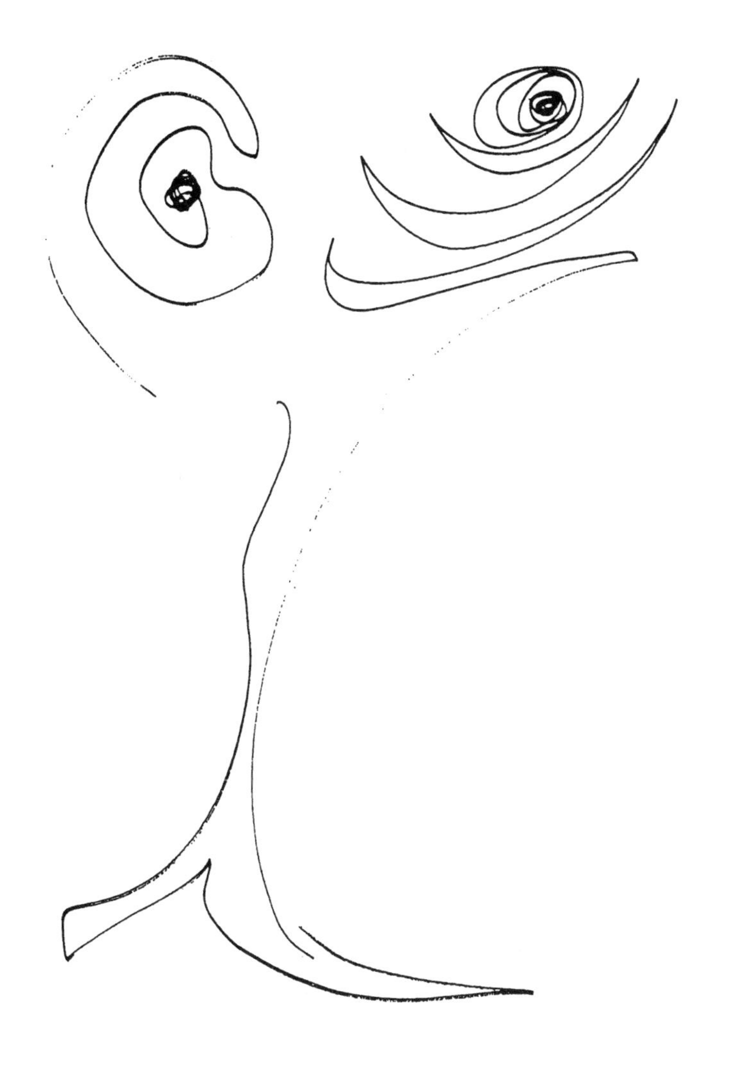

It's not only that
I'm afraid of things that go
bump *in* the night. It's more
that I just don't trust
the universe.

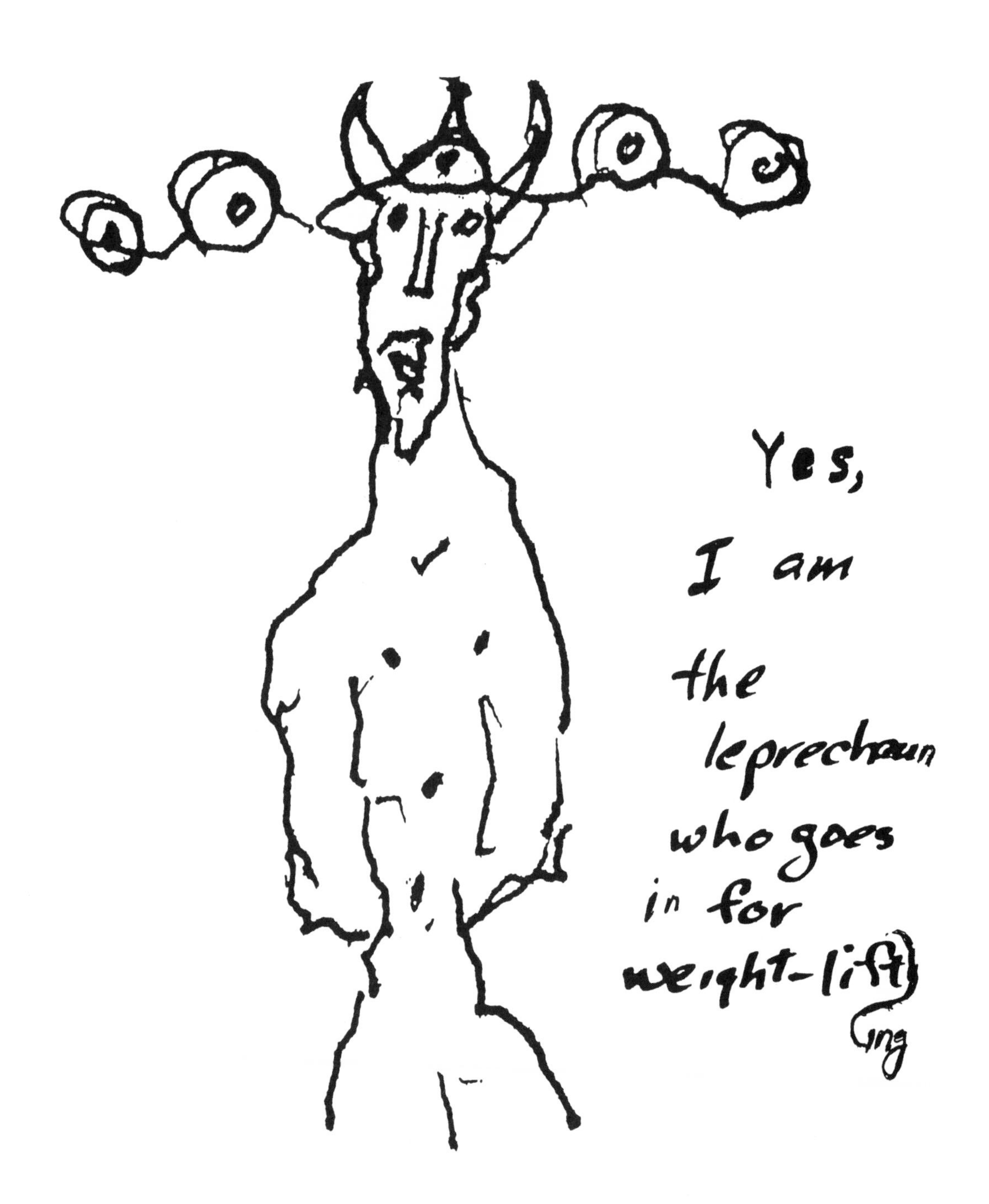
Yes,
I am
the
leprechaun
who goes
in for
weight-lifting

I have reason to believe
that the occult is on
its way back

BEWARE

I don't mind
a party that
gets
a little rough
but did you
have to throw
up
in my foyer?

Despair never
said the
drunk,
I'll pick
it up
I'll really
pick it up
because I don't
believe
in leaving
my leavings
at a lady's
door
when she's a lady
like you
you crappy
old
unhappy
bag of an armpit
anyone ever
say
you're beautiful
said the drunk as he fell on his nose
trying to kiss lady and her fortune.

# II

# Maladies of Centralists

She believed
in the
efficacy
of patterns
So she worked
on the
Avenue
of the
Madison
and
sold
glop

The steel
and
glass
of some womb
that
lacked
the love
to
give her eyes

This ill
whose
first
symptom
is
a
monotony
of nights

## UNITED CITIZENS PROTEST

Gather
me
a
monotony
of
names

Putting up
with
something
you don't
like
and calling
it charming
spells
age-in-the-face,
dear,
said
the
skin
graft
as it
said
hello
and moved into its new home
on the neck

## Therapy

People
who
despise
themselves
wear
dingy
under-
garments
said
the
psychiatrist
flinging
the sorrows
of his
seed
out, off, and away
into a
white
linen
hand-
kerchief
with a
hand-
rolled
edge.

Repetition<br>
    kills the<br>
    soul<br>
for its offers<br>
    dull the<br>
    hole<br>
    of memory<br>
where life<br>
            was once<br>
            a tree<br>
            nestling the root<br>
            with gyres<br>
                of sky<br>
            and<br>
                midnight's<br>
                murmuring<br>
                summer.

A plague is
coming
named
Virus Y S X
still unsolved
promises to be
proof
against
antibiotics
psychotherapy
Internet ventures
mega-vitamins
ATMs
celebrity diets
pundits
cell phones
foundations
cruise ships
rehab
spas
Viagra
anthrax
Botox
Prozac
breast enhancement
liposuction
insider trading
political correctness
and
even a good piece
of rare

When that unhappy day
comes to America
let Islam
take over.
The best defense is
infection.

As it grows,
the flower
breaks
through the stone.

It has yet
to prove
itself
against
the clay.

Gray without grace
day.

I'm not afraid of what lies ahead. Are you?

## Togetherness

My flesh must smell like an old tire
my sex is bitter and gone
my days are leafless and all sleep
        said the housewife
        going to the specialist
one knows what kind

but in the waiting room
she was racked by a plague
from the pots of the American
        miasma—our magazines,
        and so lady murmured
                        too quietly
even for her mind to hear:

*Reader's Digest,* please save *your* soul
and leave mine free to contemplate
eternity which must be more
        than I glimpse for myself now
        an endless promenade
across a field of baked old beans
        a cataract of dishwater
        regurgitated by the memory
of champagne I never drank
        and kings I never kissed

I want
to serve
my
Country.

## Commuter Pool

Each time I think of some little thing
I can do to get ahead,
                                        I feel as if
a foul fierce art from the nightmares
of constipation, the flaming waste of
stagnation
               (Chime! Chime! the Vowels!)
has forced its way
                                    up up into my brain
and played the lyre from Hades' heart.

So I say to myself (I am growing deaf,
my dear) I say to myself: Boy,
you are getting ready to trade
the possibilities of the future,
otherwise known as soul,
                                            for the ego,
the beans and the booze
        Remember: that Guy died for us.
But oh those dreams and how they burn.
        oh those dreams and how they burn.

Heaven cannot have a bitch
so royal as the root of my sweet itch.

# III

# Levels of Procurement

# Sex in the High Schools

Johnny
what
can I do
said the
girl
I gotta pee

She was in a
strange pad
three hours long

Why just
come here,
princess,
said
Johnny
and I'll lead you
to the throne
who serves as sink.

Oh, Johnny
said the girl
you're funny.

## Night Club

The call girl
walked along
the bar
escorted by
a plump
virile
pomaded
hip businessman,
minor league Mafia,
and behind them
trailed a smell
of stale
sulphur.

O sex
you are dying
I know
but in
whose name?
and for what
cause?

Do your duty
said I
to the beauty
as she turned
from love
(the act)
and sauntered
down the
hall
to
commune
with porcelain,
fluorescent light
and hound's sigh
of lavatory water
languishing
after the
souls
my beauty
chose
to taste
and flush
away.

Lie down with dogs
you rise with
figs
said the lady
who was the loveliest
of all my pigs.

Call this poem
the Market Place
cried
the red hair
Negress
who ball my ace.

Whores,
I prate,
make no ditties
of my sores,
for a pimp
who shows no limp
in the gait
of his will
has escaped
all ill.

I'm tired of feeling
like a parking meter
said the sad street
whore.

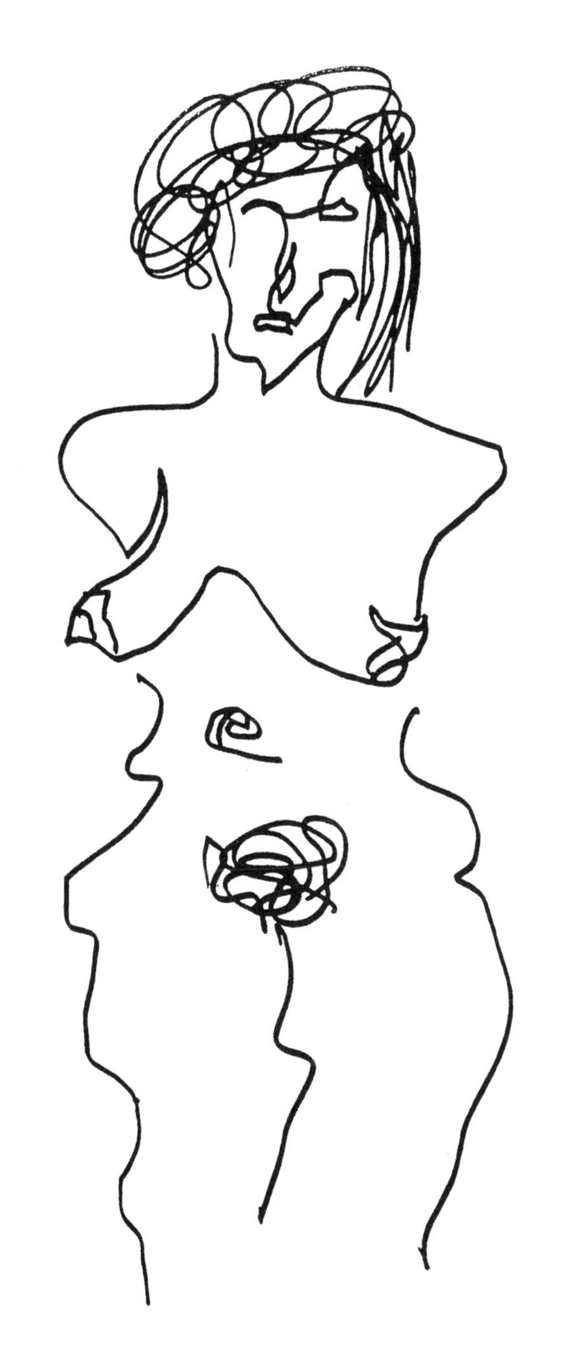

What did you expect?
The Mona Lisa?

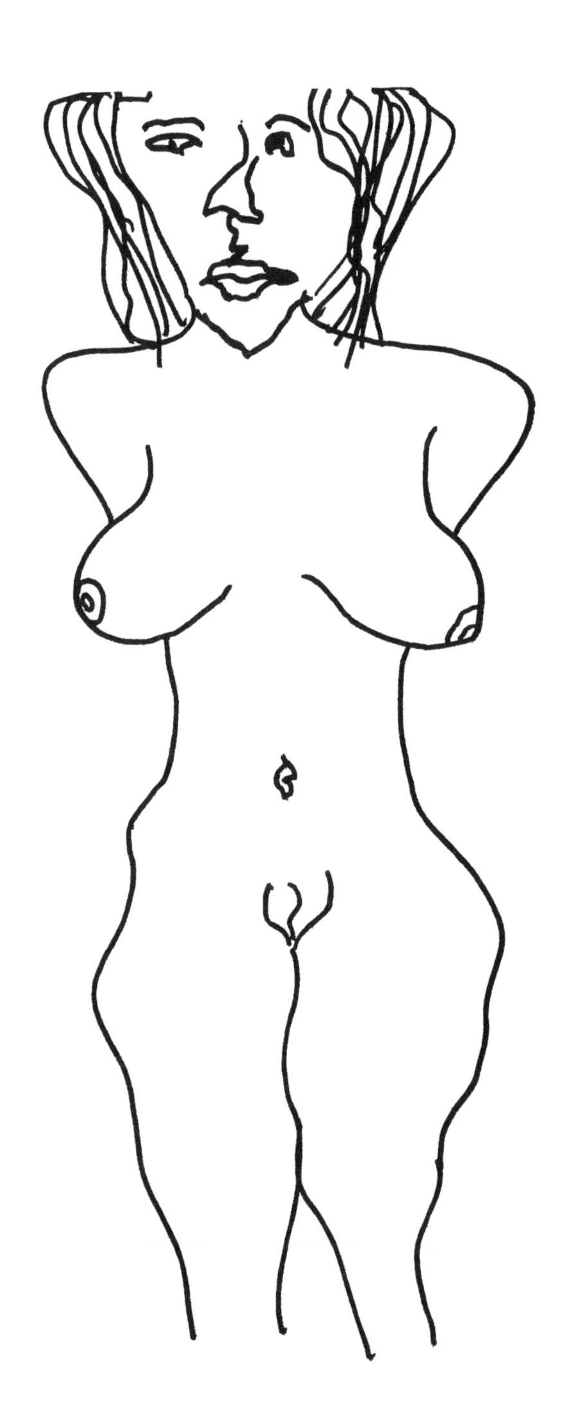

Yes, I'm Mary,
Mary Magdalene, yes.
Why are you looking
for me?

# IV

# The Mediocre

We live in a world filled with all the wonderful things

which did not happen
all the passion never born
when the sperm sailed into the sheet
and left a quiver of empty arrows

(did your little womb go pitty pat pat
when midnight passed and I wasn't there?)

We walk in cities filled with second choice
you and me planned by calculation of the budget

those neon signs cold compromise
to cheat the savage dream of fire
you do not control the flame
until you put it under glass

(all those lovely modern shacks
fifty stories of steel and mass
second choice in a new idea)

Is it better that prisons look like public schools
and airports shake their hips in plastic luxury?

What a world of second choice besets the eye
no wonder I am going blind says the Lord
and oh that static in my ear

(must everyone speak in an accent
borrowed from another and all
food die a second death?—freeze my juices
seal my flesh.)

Devil torture me no longer, I will join
the vibration in the computer chip
second choice of the wind when
the spirits of the dead failed, you
hear, to make us feel their hurt.

## Static

Dah dit dit da dit dit dah
dah dah dit dit dah dah
dah dit dit dah dit dit dah
dah dah dit dit dah dah

Mentally cool and bright
Arms fly is the war song
Father of strong in your nave

Dum ditty, dum ditty, dum
  dah dah dit dah dit dit

Bold old gold is the grave
    which does not slay
    but reduces
    the best and worst
    to mediocre

    dit dit dah
    dah dah dit

    the mediocre

Superhighways
cut through
profit and
passion
and so
inhabit
the moon
before we've
learned
its mountain
road
which
winds
in
slow
curves
of the
root
toward
the ore
and her nugget

1.

A short hair is the chromosome of a short
story
said the sadist, an assistant protestant
professor
of creative composition. His words danced
like genes in the gism of a hate-filled lair.

It was the air before his face
down from the burning glass
of his spectacle lens
to the razor of his mouth

Kill talent by teaching it procedure
said the sphincter of his nostril.
Doctor Category, said the hair
within his nose, you stifle me now

But I will grow in your grave like ivy
entwining myself in the orbital
locket of your skull

For I, royal hair of the rebellion
am the last of a lover's nerve
the poet lover who created you
old gray-haired sadistic dad
I am father of your categories
on the short hair.

Said the assistant protestant professor:
kill me, artist, curl your hair
into the bone of my grave
but I love your work

2.

Forgive my passion for category
I must believe that God is a tidy man
besides I will go before you
there are machines to replace me

Univac and One-Hole-Trac
They will bring death to your nerve
deeper than I ever dreamed.
Upon one another we fell sobbing

before the bitch of ice.
on came her machine. Yes, it said,
your short hair used to be the
chromosome of the short story

Now it is the fiber in fiberglass,
I gave one cry back clear back to
Coleridge on his lonely alp
for the horror of the albatross
was its malignant wings

Death we have betrayed your sting
and licked the long dry tongue of
intellection
much too long

We will die from anemia of the soul
in some plentitude of electronics
and her suburb

Who stole my false teeth?

# V

# A One Night Stand

## In the Hallway

My God,
  she said
I came
    in my
    hat

This time
   take your
     shoes off
      he said

My God,
   he said
   this time
*I* came
   in *my*
   hat

   well,
take it
   off
    she said,
I want
    to see
the baby
and how
    his hair
    will be.

You
have
one
of
the
greatest asses
in town
he said,

Is
it
extraordinary
she
asked?

No. It's excellent. Please do
stop

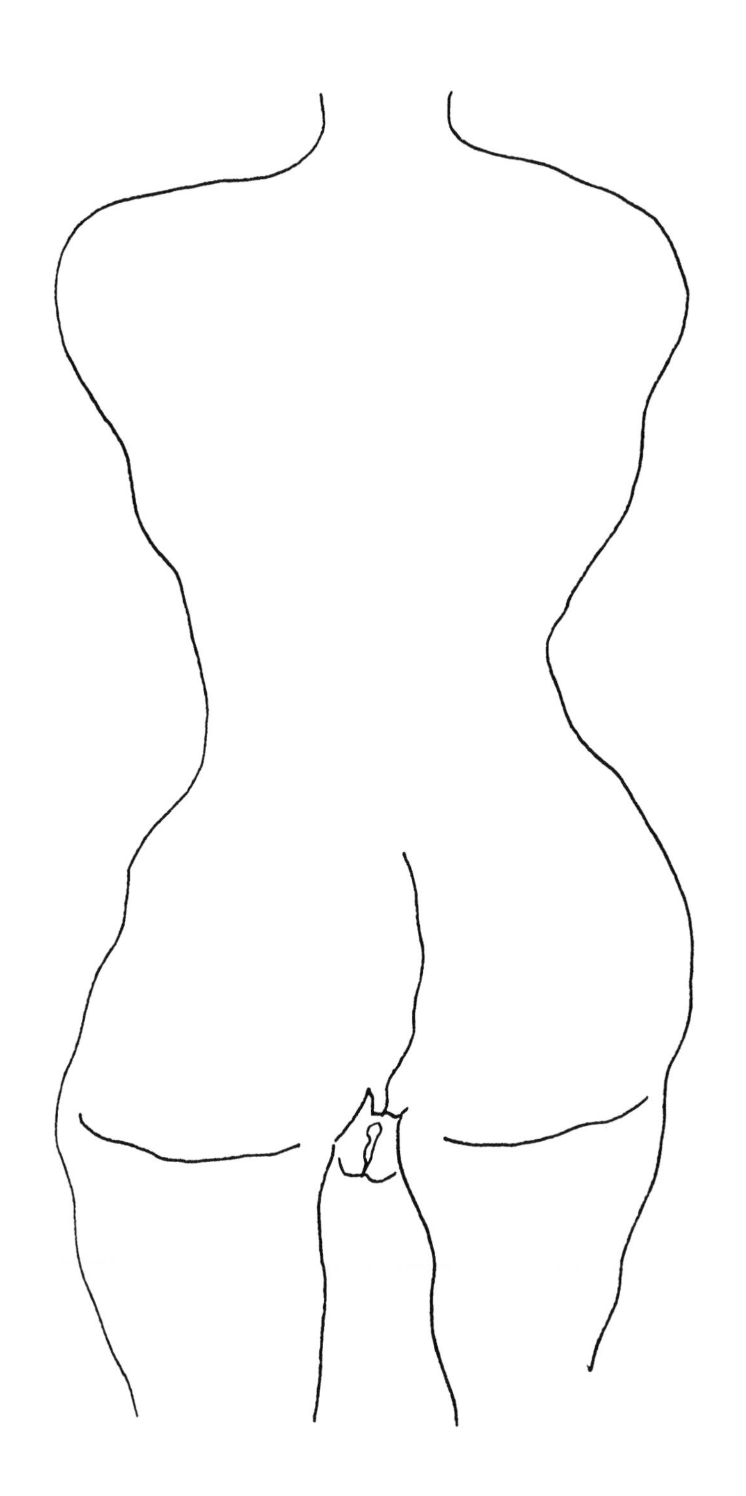

## Eating in the Kitchen

Do you have
a comb?

Use your
fingers.

## A Logic of Love

Your eyes
are beautiful
said my love.

Yes said I
eyes of
mine have
seen your
breast
and so are
beautiful
(but one's heart
was immersed
in that
calculus
of the soul
that measures
the profit
and cost
of conversions
from beauty
to power)

Your eyes
are beautiful
said my love
and have
left
me.

You're not large enough
for a whale
and much too fat
to be a shark

Porpoise
was her reply

Sleek pig
thought the mind
of my eye

Sleek pigs
are porpoises
said she
and began to cry.

## In the Mirror Is the Reckoning

Midnight
    said
    the
    lipstick
your mascara
    is mud.

I know
    said the
    eyes
but he was
    so
    attractive
and he
ended
in the vast
    middle.

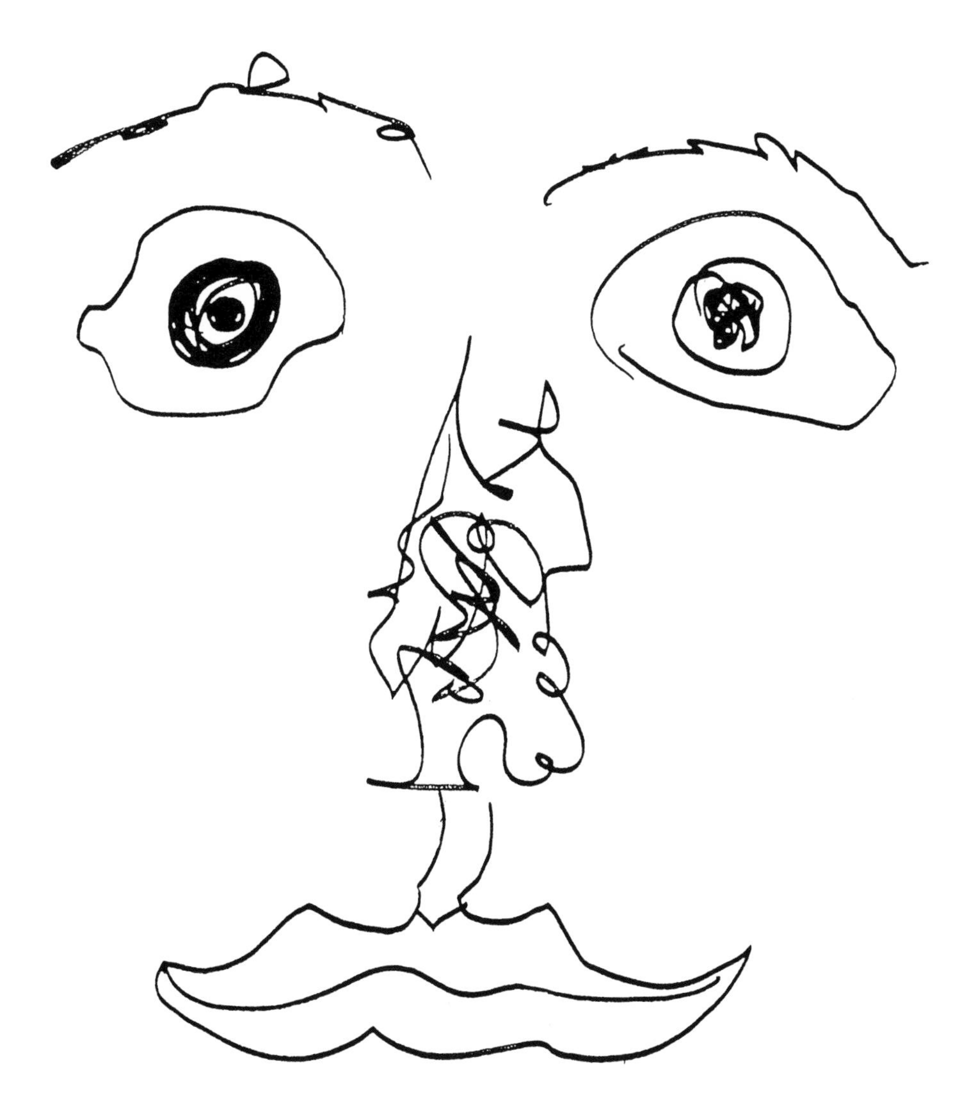

I think a bad cold is spiritual, don't you?

# VI

# Unhappy Marriage

Worry-Wart
That's how I'm
known in
my family.

What's
he got?

(made
a little
money
Lost
a little
love)

Miami.

She says
these things

I drop
like dead
meat-balls.

I want to
be a
fine
woman
and a
great
mother
to my
children
and
oh yes
you
she said

He makes love
    like a little
       pig's tail
      thought she
  all tight
   kinky
    curly cue
   and full of squeal
       why can't he
            go
   dark and deep?

Cheap!
   beep beep a beep!
   went the tail
     of the pig
roar! went the
             boar
  and with a crash
     and a snore
he went dark
     and deep
     into himself
     and sleep.

## Hallelujah!

Children
   who issue
      from
         a matrimony
         of the usual misery
         go forth
         into lives
which are best spent
         in sin
         said the Lord

You are
late
with the alimony

No more
bad news—
I beg of you.

# VII

# A Drunken Marriage

Look, she said,
he carried
her across
the street and
over the slush
why don't you
carry me?

Because you
got the curse
I got worse
we been married
ten years
and when you're
drunk you say
anything.

Whatever
dear Romeo
said
Juliet
carrying
me
across the street.

## The Good Lors

The Good Lors
gave me
my
pretty
face
The Good Lors
is full
of air
like a polar bear
with
lollypop
breeze,
daddy.

why
why daddy
why is the sky blue?
child
one would have
to embrace
your formal
Why
with coronations
of intelligence
purer than
the purest
reason
of my
heart

Gin is not water
but she is white
She makes
you very
drunk
like mommy-daddy-dolly
used to be
when she-he
fall
boom-boom
off the wagon
daddy

## Rainy Afternoon with the Wife

Wanted
without
wings
is stone
dew

Gray
without
grace
is
day
without
prey
you're
a king
with
feet
of clay

No,
lass
I'm
a
mandarin
and reached
for a
beer
first
of the
blow

You can't
have
a beer
Momma
says
no

By God
if I had a
momma
like
you
I'd
never
a
reached
the age
of six

Wanted
without
wings
is
stone
do

Gray
without
grace,
day.

Gray
without
grace,
day.

Gray
without
grace.

## Bellevue

yogurt
mart
church
for
art
blood
and
wood
is
bread
mother
menstrual
spike
and
mass

fetus
feathers
food

earning
butter
bone
and
break

fairies
father
flutes

homicide is hairy

morons murder mutes

Royal
is
the
rat who runs the race

You let everything stand
until it's knocked over
and then
you go over
and write
your own
ruins

## A Wandering in Prose:
## for Hemingway,
## November 1960

That first unmanageable cell to
stifle his existence arrived
on a morning when by
an extreme act of the will
he chose not to strike his
mother. Since this was
thirty-six hours after he
had stabbed his wife, and
his mother had come at a time
when he wished to see no one
in order to savor the woes
and pawed prides of his soul
(what a need for leisure
has the criminal heart), his
renunciation of violence
was civilized, too civilized
for his cells which proceeded
to revolt. But then it is
the thesis of this summary
that civilization spawns
its inner disease in every corner of
every church whose smell
is stale with the fatigues
of such devotion as lost its
memory on the long road
from ecstasy to
habit.

# VIII

# Drinking to Eternity

1.

Men
who work
at Time
have a
life expec-
tancy
which is
not long
said the
young man
from
Newsweek

2.

Those
who
bat out
the poop
for
the other sheet
don't use up
a thing
in
my scheme
of space
said the
young blood
from Yale

3.

But
in the
evenings
they met
and had
beers
together
in Irish bars
which looked
the proper hair
of fashion
askew
the type

4.

And as they drank
into
warm
spring
evenings
the remembered musk
of wood-smoke at dusk
brought
tenderness
to
liberty
and irony
to fate
and they
would
chant
a song
which went:

we
are
saving
our
pennies
to buy
a bond
to aid
the drive
of the United
Corporations of Community
who wish
to construct
a new
and improved
rest home
for the
pushers
on the
team

Boola-
boola,
boola-
boole.

1.

I'm rich
said
Irish
derby
slopping
a drink
to the
floor

So I've always
missed
the pleasures
of the poor.

Taste his spit!
said the sawdust
it's a scandal
and a shame

Naught but outer limbo
said the roach
on his way
on his fraught-filled
way to the door
and toward the
stair
of his own.

2.

When he reached
the cracked enamel
in the kitchen
of his pad
he made a
tour
of quarters
leaving
molecules
like pennies
on the oil cloth
of the
poor—
five molecules
of scotch
to every
plate

But the fumes had drunk
his mind to stuff
and roachie slept
an emperor's sleep
dreaming of previous lives
in derby hats
when he had slopped
the whiskey
to the floor
crying for the pleasures
of the poor.

There's one thing about you,
baby
    said Sir Cirrhosis,
of all the witches I've known
you're the merriest
        and he died
                        with style.

He died with style
        said the witch.

Yes,
    said the wind
    which rose from
    the gin
give him honor in Hell.

When I was
your age
twenty
seven
a dame
could
say
I'll put
a curse
on
you.

On!
I would say
put a curse
on me
and wonder
why
my voice
would break.

not you
but your cure
do I fear
Oh my love
for your cure
is a
curse
upon me.

## Bar Twists

I await her
hot-breathed
cigaretted
garlicky
version
of all the lost days.

Cheer up
whispers she
(silently)
hugging
the other
mugger.

Hurts me
loathe chicks
wife
did me in
I cannot
forswear
to gaze
said the rage.

Other drunks spit.
Creepy girls giggle.

## Epitaph of a Rail

I used to drink
until six
  in the morning
so I could make
    dames
and now I drink
until six
  in the morning
watching other
    guys
  make dames.
  Eheu Fugaces.
Which means:
  Fuck aces!
  before the fleeting
  years go by

I am washed
by the sorrows
of love

I gave my soul to him.

# IX

## Intermission

(During the Intermission
There Will Be a Variety Show)

## Ian Fleming Revisited

I had a spider once
and fed it neon tubes
until its web did gleam
like Las Vegas in the dawn
Roulette I used to call her
and the spider
drinking dew from grapefruit rind
to oil the knees
would smile and say:
every Roulette has her croupier.

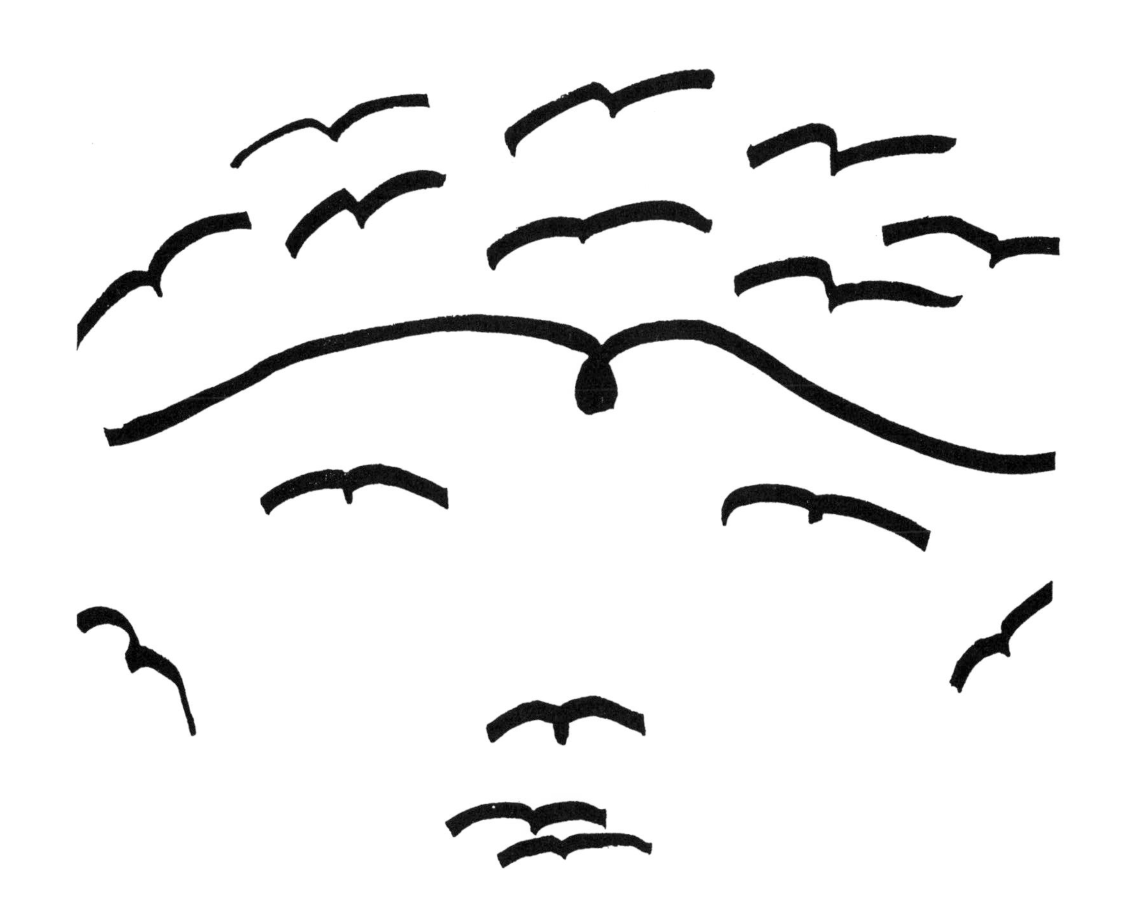

A bird just pooped on me!

On Me, too!

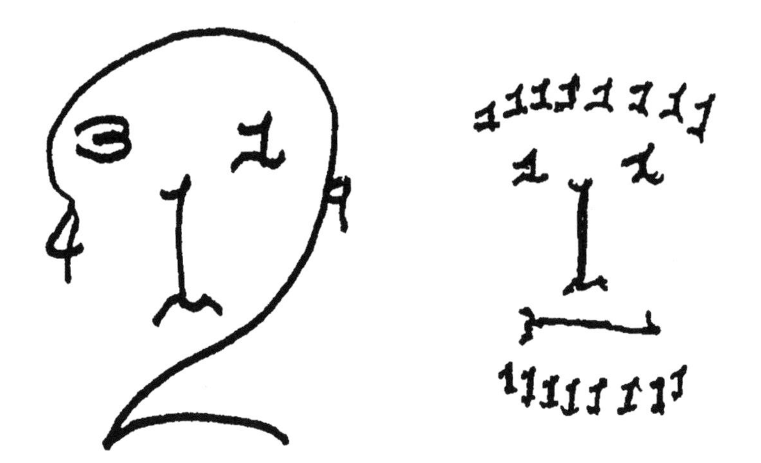

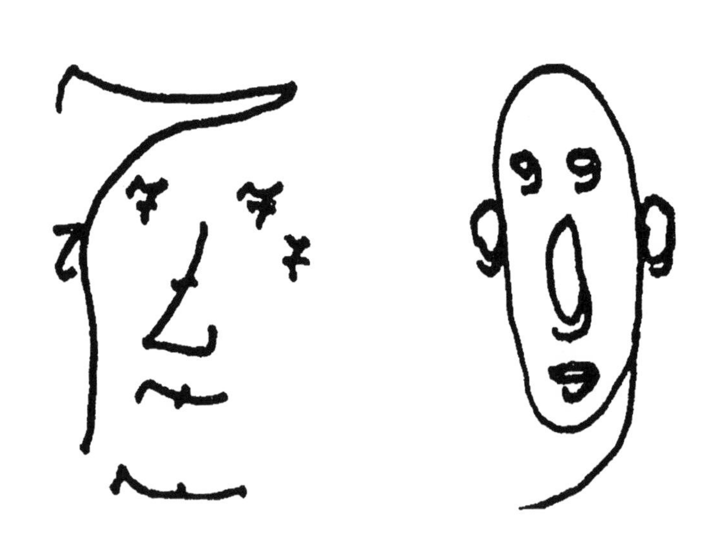

"Petals on a wet black bough."

More petals

My head is in
a whirl.
I just can't do
arithmetic.

I was supposed to be a baker's dozen.

## Sports Channel

Does the football team
eat a lot?

Oh, I think so, Jim
those football
boys are
are pretty big
down there.

I sure remember
when you
two titans
last met
last November.

So do I.
That fateful
gray day
in Green Bay.
The weather was
so bad we almost
stayed in our
hotel and ate each other.
Our boys were
keyed-up, I tell you.

Let's
stamp out
bad dialogue.

That's *your* problem
said the
toad.

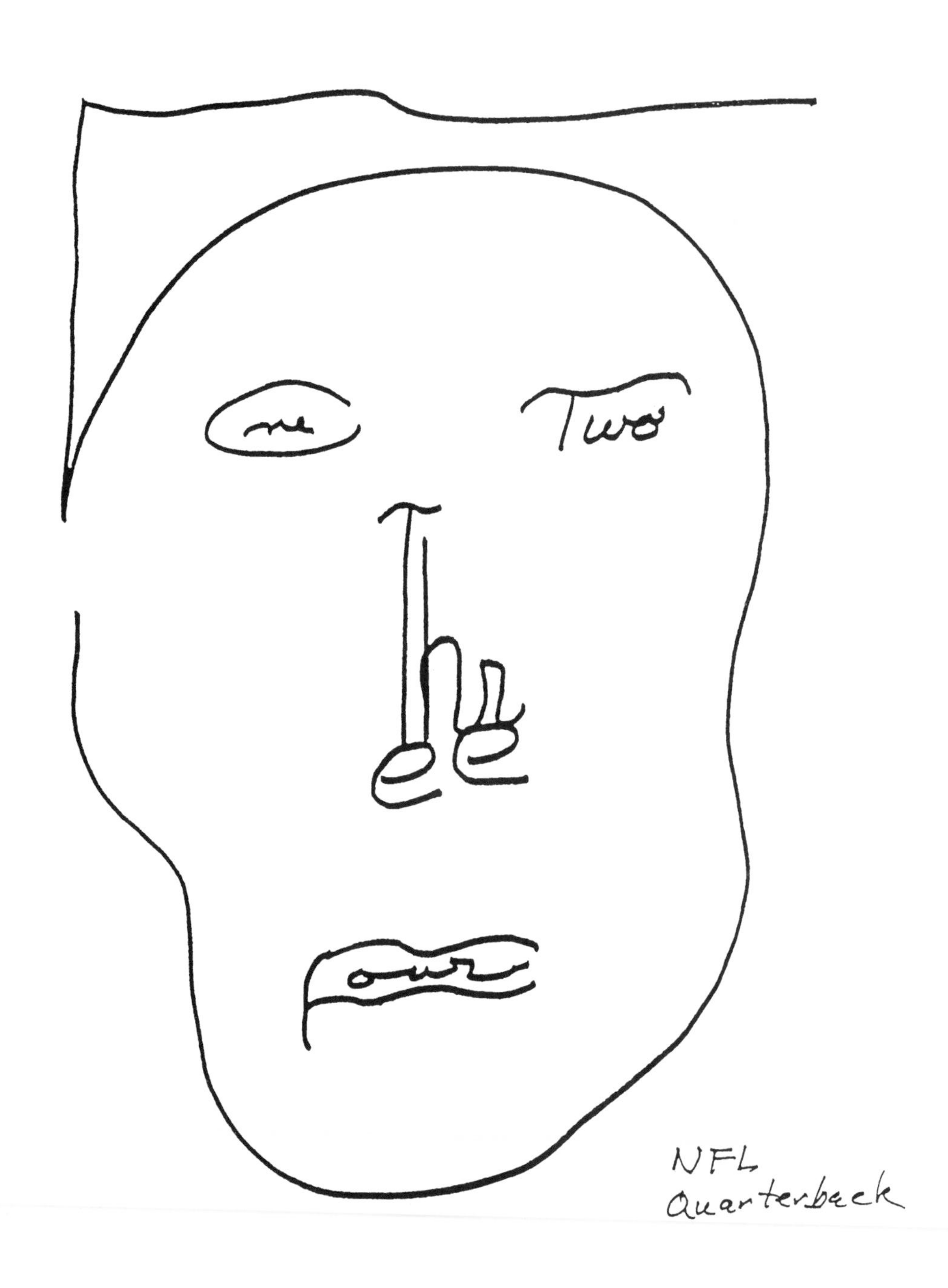
one
Two
three
four
NFL
Quarterback

High
School
Quarterback

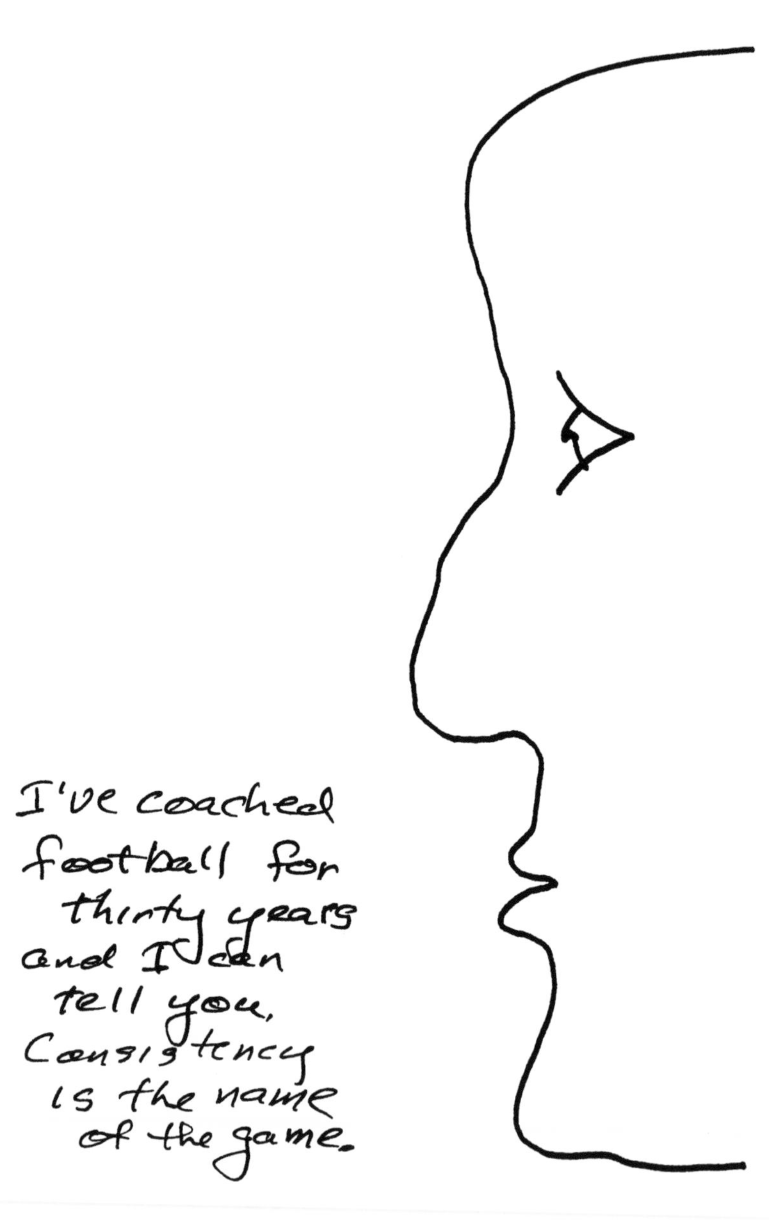
I've coached
football for
thirty years
and I can
tell you,
Consistency
is the name
of the game.

Yes sir, this is
my third year
in the Pro Bowl.

## Illumination

why do
    you
    always
    have
        to
        go off
        on a
            tangent
        said his mother.
why can't you
            be
            nice
            and
            clean?
Look!
            Your handkerchief
                has a hole in it.
            Let me give you a
                new one.

Don't you dare.
This way
    I can
    blow my nose
    and see what's
    going on
            said Rimbaud
            at six.

the worst to be said
about mothers
is that they
are prone

to give

kisses

of con-
grat-
u-
lation

that make you feel
like a battleship
on which someone
is breaking
a bottle

Bar Mitzvah in the Suburbs

# X

## A. Interplanetary Is Trans-temporal

So, I said
to Aeschylus:
"You don't
understand
the nature
of
Greek drama."

He's gone the moment I get him in my sights.

Picasso said that the act of meeting me when he was a very young man was one of the most exceptional and determining events of his life. I concur.

PICASSO SAID
THE
EXACT SAME
THING
TO ME!

Where can I
find a man
who is my equal?

That Salome!

Portrait of Picasso

as Salvador Dali

Of course,
Mr. President,
we
are
indeed hot
on
the track
of the
wonder
disease

and
are
now feeding
tetra-phenomenase
its dose.
Expect to save
it
and all
genome
compounds
if the
Internet
does not collapse.

release
the anger
contained
in a fart

and there'll
be power
enough
to reach
the moan

said the
physicist
as he
assumed
the throne

I mean
the moon.

# B. In Which We Visit the Abductionally Challenged

The aliens did abduct
me, but I still feel
more or less intact.

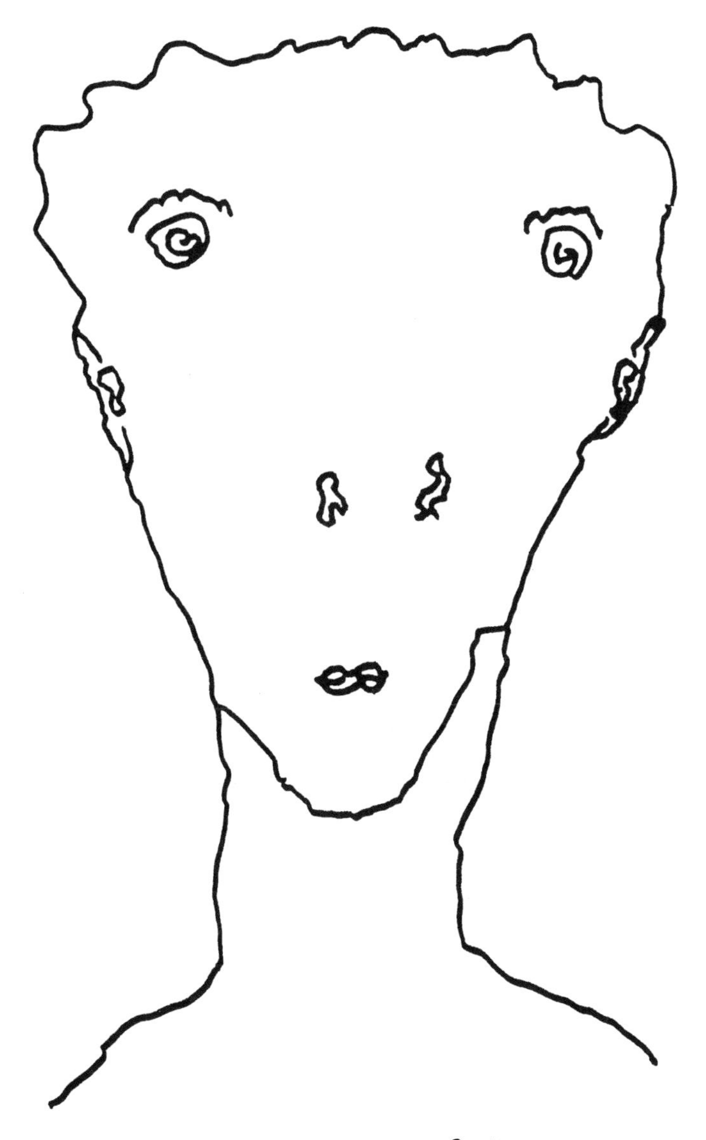

I CAN'T SAY
THE SAME

It was unspeakable

SEINFELD

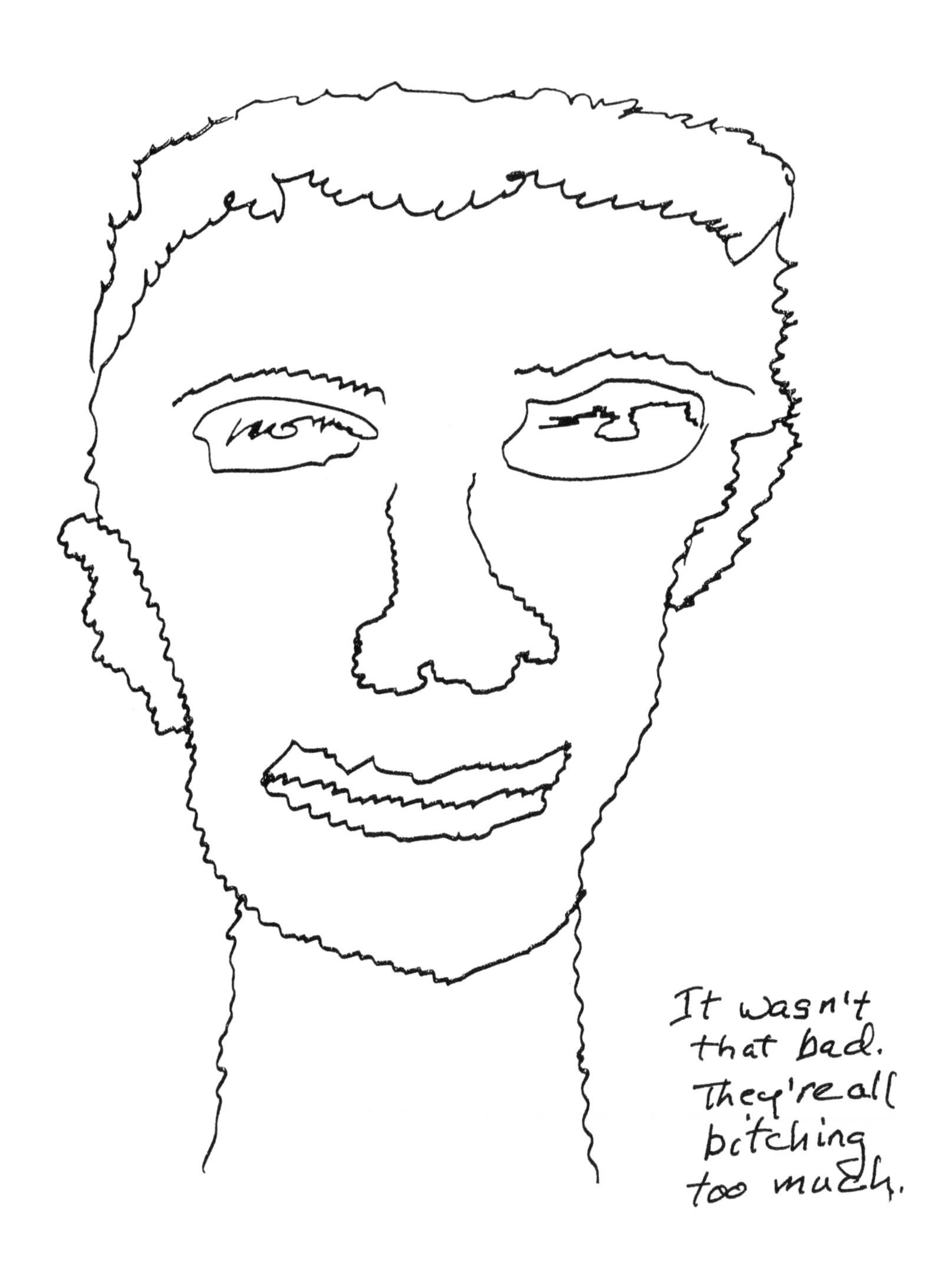
It wasn't
that bad.
They're all
bitching
too much.

Believe it or not
I had a romantic
interlude with
one of them.

Seven

one two six

8 three Nine

Four

5

I can't complain. Their interest in me was scientific.

earthpeople
assume
that I am
trying to
hypnotize them.
I just wish to
understand
what they are up to.

# XI

# The Upper Classes

## A. Transatlantic

The Prime Minister said:
The higher a man rises
the more he must
dissemble
until he
can no longer
detect his own lies
of course by then
everything
that seems good
betrays me
and everything
which makes
me warm
tastes foul.

Money
is a
river
flowing
downhill
over
hills
of
character
in the
rich

The secret of money
is that you have to
know how to allow
it to grow.

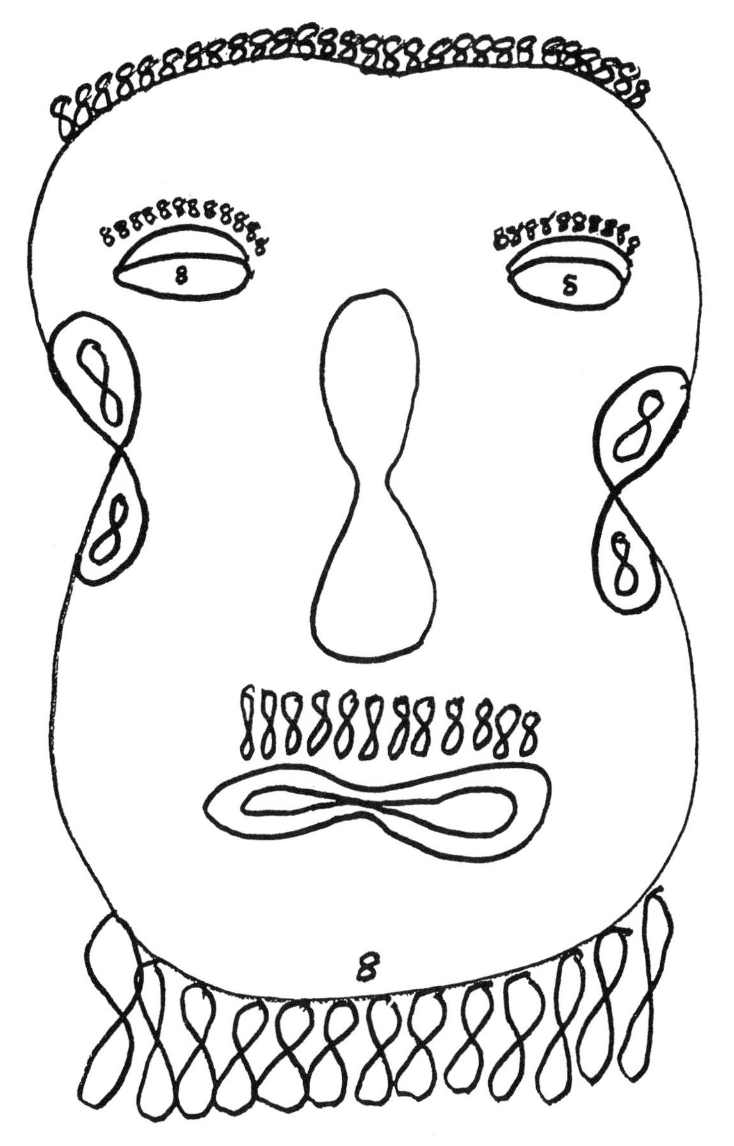

They call me Robber Baron
Go, figure!

## Registers

You must meet her.
She's rather nice.
she's an
absolute
brigand
who came out
of a whorehouse
in Baltimore.
Then she married
a Jewish man
from Macy's
And then my father.
Now she has
the most terrible
dining room
in New York.
It's all gold.
Last year
she finished
decorating her house
and charged
one thousand dollars
a plate
to let people in.
No drinks.
Of course
it was for
a marvelous charity
called Baskets
For people
without
arms
or legs.
Isn't that nice?

## The Socialite's Song

I love Bobby, Bobby's divine
The Windsors came to
see him
and the Duke
kept calling for
Bye Bye Blackbird
over and over again.
It was a glorious night.
I borrowed mascara
from the Duchess
before we were done
we were crying
so hard
even the Duke.
How were we to know
that the West
Old World
would shiver from blight
and I would turn
to a Prince
of the Congo
saying: embrace me
darkest delight
for in your firmament
are stars.

Oh blackbird
do not banish us
banish not
the lovers
of Bobby
when he sang
Blackbird
bye-bye
for can it be
we heard
the chord
of the cannibal
sharpening his knife
on a blooded stone
and wept for you
as well as us.

Young winners
make weak old losers
said Bobby
removing his mask
to show
he was now
King
of our
Congo.

## Definition of a Lady

She grasps
the root
while kissing
the bud

## Definition of a Hero

He
thrives
in
dikes

Evil
fingers
up
and
down
my
spine
remind
me
that
sex
is
not
always
divine.
But
sometimes
it is
with
the most
astonishing
collection
of
horrible
people.

## Ode to a Lady

Cold and swinish are your crafts
Mean and nasty, foul your arts
The spirit of a lover you would never kill
'Tis tastier far to deaden him.
Yes, maggots are your pets
and garlic your bouquet

Cold and swinish are your crafts
a pestilence on me
For I have primed my iron
in your lore and now
your faults revealed
my eyes are blinded still
by the image of a woman
who is a virgin to my touch
and never smiles the lover's dirty grin
of sweets we shared
and share we will again

No, you are a work of art
pristine, inviolate,
shiver of midnight away
from the touch of my tip all
fingers stretched

You call to artists
in other lands
singing sweetly:

Create me
dear singing loin
of some manly harp
create me
for I stifle where I stand
and lady-like
must drown the moment
in the lake of much too many
who leave me lazy like a snake
So, create me, dear man,
beyond my eye.

And I answer:
  snake and foulest bitch
  swine of a hundred feet
  I am your artist across the seas
    and love you, heart,
    because you are purer far
    than all your arts
      and all your swilling crafts,
    purer far because your heart
      dared to call
      when others—
      cats, grand dames,
      fraises fatales,
      and all the avaricious humps
      could think of nothing
        but flight from me.

      Come back,
       says piggy
      Can it be, poor harp
        Can it really be
      that you are the voice
                  across the sea?

      Yes, come back, says swine-song in your heart
      Come back, come back, come back
      For names you've called me
            far and wide
      Wine of a hundred feet
            Sweet lord you're kind
      Yes come to me honey-bee
            and I will kill you.
      Over here my lad,
            God, you're bad.

## Marriage à la Mode

Cook for him?
Of course not.
We eat out
  all the time.
He's gotten fat
He's gotten
    very
    fat
    *longing*
  for good
    cooking
    said the Bitch
  in a voice
    of absolute
    tenderness for Mr. Bitch
    curious fellow
    her husband.

## Devils

One of us
will
be
better
looking
when it's
all
over.

# The Upper Classes

## B. Witches and Warlocks

The most
eligible
bachelor
in London
is a category
conceived
by presumptive
witches
weary
of doing
without
their widow's weeds—
whispered
the epigram
to the boutonniere.

Go fix the flowers fuck-face
was the King's reply

I'm fast
  becoming
  a goose
    said the bitch
    blinking her eye
    to the beat
      of my
        intent
        light, deliberate and dry

I hate to have a ball
    which goes de trop said I

De trop, or not de trop
    dare your
    deliberations
    go deeper
      ducks.
    for love
      which is light
      and dry
      makes me think of money
        and her dirty bucks.
        So waltz me
    around again Willie
    hard dark and deep
    the keys to the dungeon
          are buried
    in mummie's
    murderous
    keep.

You bruise
  my
  catatonia
  said
    the saint
    to the witch
  after he had
    fallen
    so far
   as to nod
    assent
    to a
    shitty suggestion

Is that all
  asked the witch
  accoutomé ma foi
    to eat the shit
    of the
    superior.

The saint forgave her
  and kissed a sore
  content with the
    notion
   it came from mort.

Deep in my dungeon
  I welcome you here
Deep in my dungeon
  I worship your fear
Deep in my dungeon
  I dwell.
I do not know
  if I wish you well.

Deep in my dungeon
  I welcome you here
Deep in my dungeon
  I worship your fear
Deep in my dungeon,
  I dwell
A bloody kiss
  from the wishing well.

## The Ride of the Sad Saint

1.

The air was full of curses
looking for no fight.
The devils and the witches
were all alone tonight
save for a saint
who was sad.

Mad, mad, you're mad,
cried a lad in the garb
of a girl
Saints are not sad
but sadistic.

Cruelty is the kindest wound
for dung, replied the saint.
Go forth and sin
in such a way
you need not run
at break of day.

Not one said yea.
Still, the saint merely sighed
he knew a saint
must not aspire
to the courage of a god
nor try too long
to bear such pain.

Besides, the saint was vain.
It was the drop life left
in his humility
in the couloirs of his humility
in the catatonia of his senility
in the crease of Carmen's ear
in the crease of Carmen's ear.

I am brave by an act
of will, said the saint
my nature is to fear
O saint even you must fear
the crease of Carmen's ear.

2.

For Carmen is a cutthroat
Carmen is a queen
Carmen sings of passion
and blows her breath at me.

Carmen is a royal whore
Carmen is a slut
Carmen has a mustache
and smiles at flowing blood.

I knew Carmen when she was young
Before her mustache bleached
A colored flag around her neck
she kissed the pirate's fleet
and seduced herself to me
and stole from me a steed.

Her head upon the pillow
she caught her flesh to mine
And went off at a gallop
some galley's keep to find
presenting me her ear
returning greed a fiend.

Oh, I was a young man
Cold, evil and strong
And few were the ladies
I couldn't dog, dog-
bitch, you're in my bed
and cue them out half-dead.

3.

Five children started in my land
Six across the sea.
None knew my hand upon
his head. Royal bastards all.
One swore my death was in
her vow. Loyal bastards royal.

But Carmen was a crueler siege
Than all my evil gathered
And tore the heart right out of the ram
while all that's vain was shattered.
And now I am a saint. (O pity me.)
Now I am a saint. (O pity me)

I stare into the eyes
of devils,
devils dark and foul
and look them down
and steal their ground
while in me tolls a hollow
by the heart
of Carmen's ear
near the heart of Carmen's ear
that scar on horror's breast
which fears no fire
for death to Carmen is Devil's dare
for Hell to Carmen is heaven's mare:

a trot away from this flat world
where saints and witches stale
and war's too whored for open fight
swears the heart of Carmen's ear
swings the hooves of Carmen's steed:
ride, ride, ride with me.

4.

Come ride with me into my land
Down down along my crease
And we will live forever
    in the marrow of the beast
    and we will live forever
    in the sweetmeat of desire
Oh we will live forever
    In the sweetmeat of disease
    oh we will live forever
    by the steeps at Carmen's knees
    we will live forever
in the crease of Carmen's ear
in the crease
in the crease
in the crease of Carmen's ear.

# The Upper Classes

## C. Camembert and Caviar

It's a fine wine
hearty as one drinks it,
peppery
yet it seems
to come
florid
and
soft

Yes, I answered,
we have an
old peasant
saying:
It's a fine wine
but the devil
pooted
in it
once.

The second bottle
was
Sierra Blanca
a California
Sauterne,
with a moldy
label
and a green
rusted cork,
age and
color
of
cobweb.
So we
chose it
over a fast
dry
cool
professional
blonde
from
Bordeaux.

Yet when
the
nectar
crested
over
the eddies
of fume
that rose
from
the dust
of the cork,
the wine
was sour
and
squalid
like
bad breath
on a good goose
with bad teeth.
Oh well,
we murmured
never fall
for a
pretty face
again.

Nonetheless, we agreed: Domestic may be the wisest choice
For the ocean voyage spoils the wine.
It is the movement of the waves upon
the memory of a grape
Water lapping water is too sensual to the touch
wine delivers its love to the bottle
before the trip is out.
Ohhhh. Unhappy continent
livid America
the taste of wine, of foreign wine that crossed the sea
is like a taste of love the second time.
Poor wine said Lady Grape shedding a tear.

Vodka is fine
we agreed,
one can keep
one's character,
it doesn't do
funny things
to the style
of the soul
departing,
it doesn't
get into
the end
of one's
fingers
and leave them weak.

You must never let
anything
get into
the end
of your fingers
but
        Love
said evil
getting up
to get another drink.

The caviar is marvelous, however.
(I do love the taste of the soul
in each little egg.) Still!
One does have to entertain the thought
that learning so much about the deep
                                        perhaps,
oh dear God no,
perhaps next life
I will be a fish.

fizz
fire
flash
foo
flesh
    went the bubbly.

Como no, Senor
    said the sommelier
    I know some fine
    accommodations
    in the sea.

If poetry is the food of the soul
then some poems are like pot roast
lots of meat, pannikins of gravy and
a great deal of taste all very
much the same.

Other poems are fishy
tang, pepper, weed, and green as the
sea. I know a few which stick to the
fingers. Poetaster in patis-
serie. But my poems—
I want my poems
to be like bones. Bones make it possible
to stay in good form.
And there are
poems which taste of grass, air, earth,
rock salt and old lady granite in the
minerals (not to mention all
the dairy products, milky poems,
vegetables and gourds.)

But I want
my poems to be like bones and shine
silver in the sun.
For poems which
are like bones crackle in my teeth.
Look for the death within the death.

Since Camembert is the King of cheeses
foul, corrupt, redolent of old uses, dirty royal feet
and wealth beneath the ground,
then Brie becomes my Prince
said the air of morning to her appetite.
Still, said Camembert, monarchies produce architecture,
princes bastards
and morning speaking to her appetite is mud
to those who drink with Faust at night
Yes, adventurers gargle the sour blood of dukes
and eat me says Camembert
Power is nothing without the smell
of a royal crevice at your finger.
Oh, says Brie, nothing is so lovely
as the milk of morning on my mouth.
Do not let the world sodden us with its liver,
its poor colon and a smell of the hoarded past
Good architecture comes from young men
stealing the better half of form
from the royal round rump of some majestic lady
who smuggles jewels to the prince
and embezzles deeds from the King.

One cannot give a funeral service to the fart
and yet there are broken winds that walk the plank in pride.

## Hymns

The sweetest
song
I ever heard
was
the sound
of each
tongue
on the
other's
bung
said a choirmaster
for the Devil.

It's not easy
to be a priest
these days.

## The Inaugural Ball

1.

There was a time
when fornication
was titanic
and the Devil
had to work
to cheat a womb.

(pride of his teeth
on a root
long enough
to
pluck it out
the green wet sea
of the pussy slue
and down a falling
flight
of cellar stairs
hard, dark, deep
into the maiden brown
rooting out the bowels
which fell
like assassins
upon the white foam
of God's arrow)

2.

There was a time
when fornication
was satanic
and the Devil
had to work
to cheat a womb.
(licked the liqueur
of milady's loot
off a hot feathered face
and sobbed in despair
as God won the race
to shoot the fury
of his intentions
to the proper place.)

3.

But now the Devil
smokes a cigar
and has his nose
up U.S. phar-
maceutical
The assassins
who fall on God's
white arrow
give off the fumes
of chemical
killer bedded
in vaseline
as heroic
in its odor
as the exhaust
which comes off a
New York City
Transportation
System Bus

4.

I do not want
to believe it.
(Ay, no quiero verla!)
that the scent
of the clerk
at Merck
and
Merck
is the last
of the Devil's odor.

No.
I want
to declaim
that the time
will return
when
Lucifer wrestles
the Lord again
for fucking
all glory
of Heaven's vault
in flame,
and
mandarins
mad
with
fright
at fucking
and God's
black
light.

# XII

# The Lower Classes

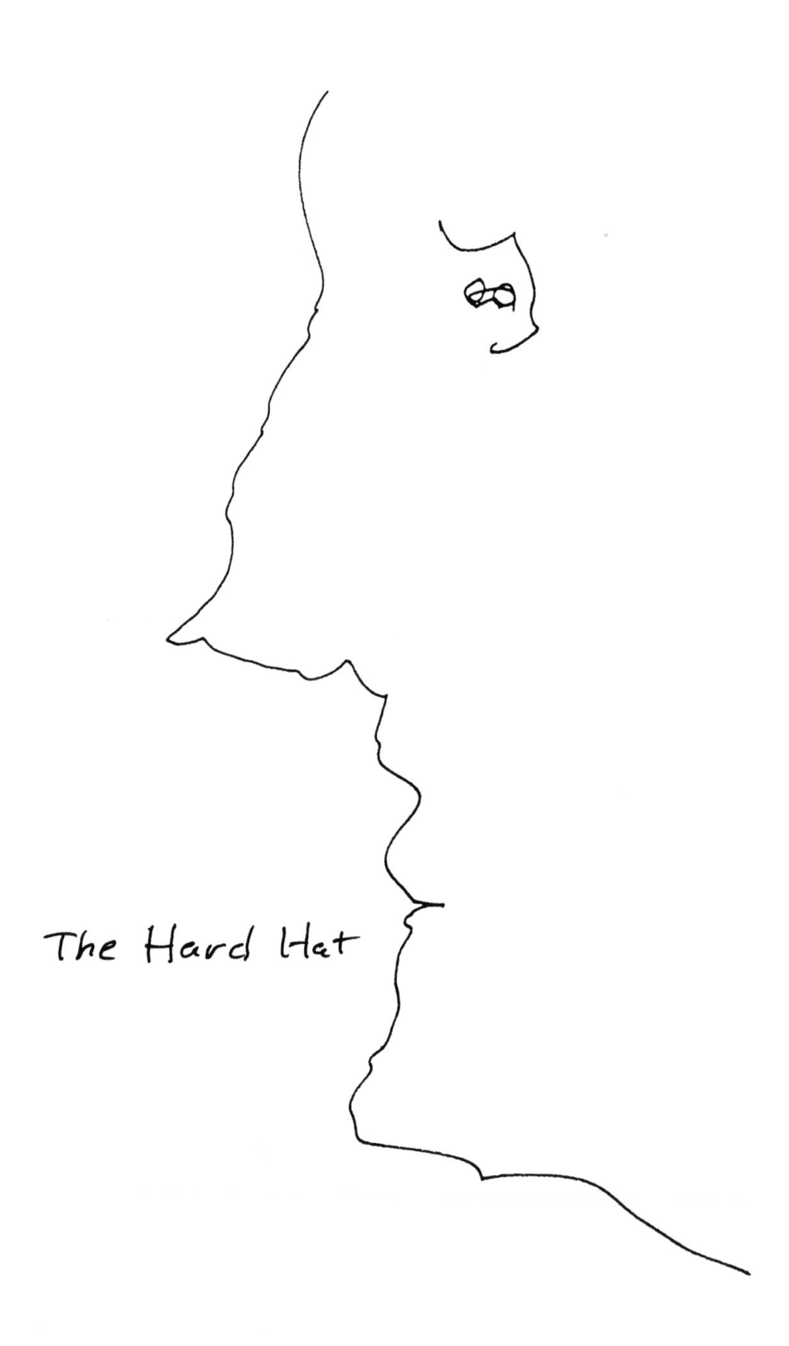
The Hard Hat

The Hard Hat's
best friend

I'm the best friend's father. And I can take both of them.

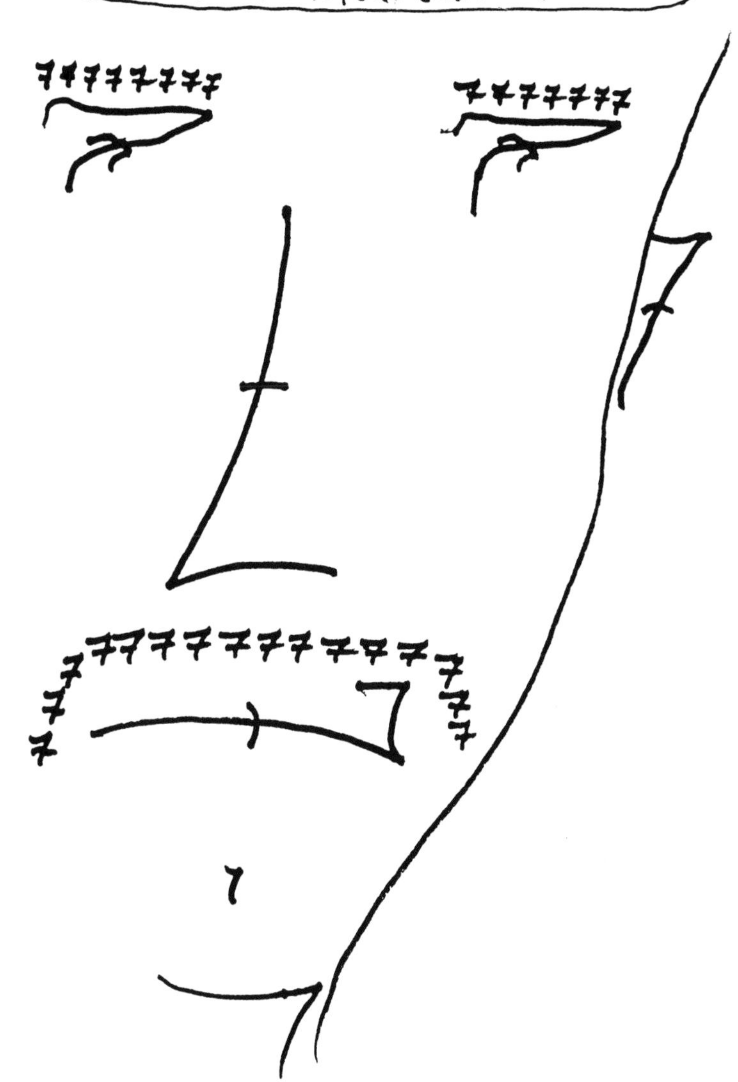
Yes I'm in the Militia. Just call me Lucky.

I know things
The Sopranos don't.

There was a meet for the boys
The moolahs the mozzers, the Maf, the Coast and the Nose
even the bonze and the dunes.
They were in to get acquaints for a new soft commodtz
and general affiliate.

How, said the Coaster to the Nostrand
do you think soft sell began?
Well, I'll tell you said the Maf; we said to the dunes
whaderya trying to shove that shit
    down people's troat for?
Slip it up their stroonz
    you asshole
Strike a match!

Said the dunes to the Maf,
Whaderya want to give me a hard-on for?
you have hurt my feels
how much can the heart of my feels take
before the heart of some other Guinea's feel
    is forced to break?
Listen, said the dunes to the Maf—you're a dunze,
Don't get hit!

So they had a ruining
They had the runs.
That was some thunder.
Those fartsaroons came close to eating all the prunes.

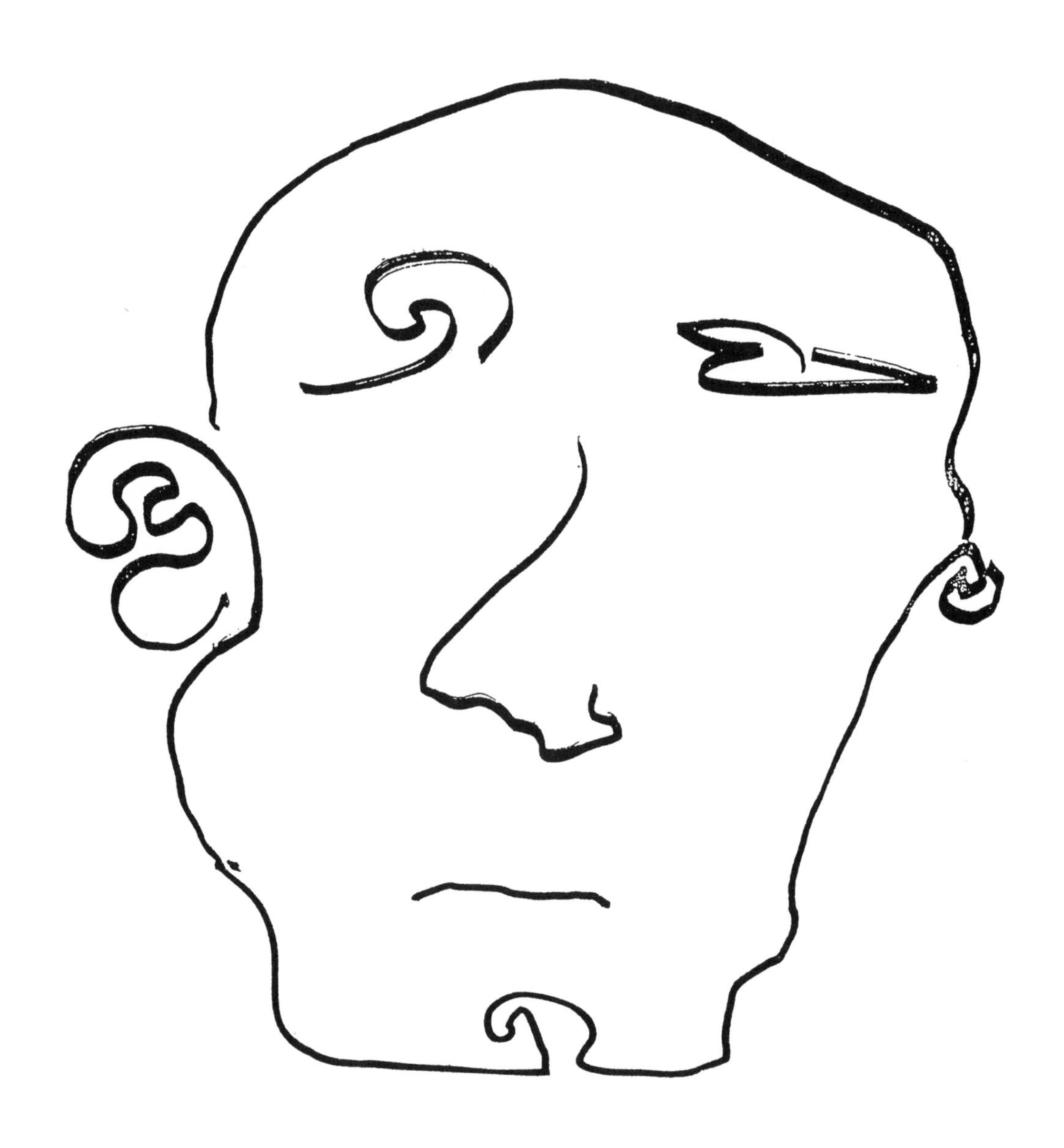

You don't know who I am
and you don't want to find out.

Ditto!

"Who says
I'm shit-face?"
said
Fuck-face
Farinacci.

I'm Ass-face—
Fuck-face Farinacci's
best friend.

KEEP YOUR NOSE
CLEAN
ASS-FACE

They ask me if I'm
the consigliere.
I tell them—keep looking!

## East Village

In New York
it's not
enough to be polite,
one must
be
brutally polite,
to wit:
variations
observe
the theme
of foul
economy
Shithead
follows
up your
bunny
honey
in
balance
and pro-
priety
Jew
bastard
if said
in a
Village
bar
is as
gentle
as
spade
creep

Fuck off
can be
returned
with
three
stiff
fingers
to the
plexus
or the neck
The
rule
is
keep
cool
This
is
New
York

Now
these
children
want me
to roast
their tea
said
The Man
with the bag

Do they
think
I'm a
mother
with
shades
and a
furled
umbrella?
Go to sea
Jim,
I have
something
in my
head
that
would
really
kill
you

## To the Ghost of Senator Joe

Another orphan
said McCarthy
let's have a high mass
and kiss her ass
before we kick
her cunt in,
sister superior.

Ooooooo
Is this poem good for the Jews?
asked Reverend Godspee
of the Inter-Faith Council
for
The Committee of
Hearth and Heart, Share and Care

Kick his cunt in too
said McCarthy
Reverend Godspee is
a Communist

You're fucking aye
said all the louts
in all the bars
in Queens
and they were right
for once.

You
*can't*
and you
*won't*
print that,
said
the Lady who
was running
for office
in a voice
that
released
half
her
souls
from prison
and
dropped
them
into
Hell.

## To the Lower Classes

Noblesse
Oblige
has one rule
and
one rule only

You must be
so nice
so bright
so quick and
so well turned
that
no one need
tell you
a second time.

Tell me what?
that the world
is well-lost
for love
and the upper
classes
are the
law above?

I tell you this:
if the
upper classes
are kin to God
in style—
(which is one hypothesis
we do not ignore:
how else account
for elegance?)

if the
upper classes
are kin to God
in style
then God has no love
but guilt, nor a style
apart from fashion,
no courage but to
do in duty
what
one does not desire
and no worth
but for His love
at beauty

For there
is noble's work
their plea:
that they
love in truth
with all sense
of Christian
love
divorced from self
the air of beauty
and her pomp.
The poor know naught
but death
they do not free
they obliterate.

Stripped of its
distinctions
life is a flat city
whose isolated spurs
cut the sky
like housing projects.
Think of the air
whose heart is bruised
by touching such artifacts.
(Does the cutworm forgive
the plow?)

I tell you, say the rich,
the poor are naught
but dirty wind
welling in air-shafts
over the cinders
and droppings of
the past, their
voices thick
with grease
and ordure,
sewer-greed
to corrode the ear
with the horrors
of the past
and the voids
of new stupidity.
One could drown
waiting for the poor
to make
one fine distinction.
Yes, destroy us
say the rich
and you lose
the roots
of God.

Destroy them
say the poor
we cannot breathe
nor give
until we etch
on their rich nerve
the cruel razor
and heartless club
of our past,
those sediments of
waste
which curbed
our genes
and flattened
the vision we
would give
the chromosome.

Yes, destroy them
say the poor
burn them, rob them
gorge their tears
and such half of beauty
lost to pomp
will flower
unglimpsed wonders
in the rose,
will flower
unglimpsed wonders
in the rows.

I wonder,
said the Lord
I wonder if I know the answer
any more.

Panhandling
the Bowery
on Sunday aft
with gray sky
and no butts
we had an
argument
over the
        merits
of frozen food
versus canned

Canned is awful,
I said, it comes
out half dead.

Yea, said Red
          but
          frozen
          is stone.

## Square Dance

On the meat of the rich
And the urge of the poor
The purge of the ore
And the grease of the bitch
A lady was burning
A whore was a-scorch
Gorge was the cheese
And ass the itch
Of Pussy and Pick-nose
And swish out the twitch
Deep hurted the liver
Raw buried the sauce
Hotshit the hurricane
Herded the gourd
Howligan, hooligan
Hurry up all
Tonight is the night
Of the Hip Hole Ball

Perfume and heart
Snatch squinch and squeeze
Ear-wax and dingle
Fuck tit and dong
Fling a hole on your point
And sweeten the joint
Tonight is the night
Of the Hip Howl Ball.

# XIII

# Hunting for Poems

Men who go out for game
hope to find in our blood
the poems of their flesh
said a deer in her pain

As a poetess, I try
to rise above flora,
fauna and gender.

Even the seeds of
sensation
are
thrilling to me.

Spleen?
Yes! Bad
poetry always
inspires spleen
in me.

Some of
my ideas
are impossible
to describe. I'm so
afraid
that people
will squash
them.

Burnt Umber
Yellow Ochre

A crap,
said
the
pedant
picking
his
paws
is an
idealist
who has
not yet decided
he is worthy
to be considered
a shit.
Mon dieu, Feinspan,
in terror, I
exclaimed
abjure the
Anglicans

*"Our concern was speech, and speech impelled us*
*To purify the dialect of the tribe*
*And urge the mind to aftersight and foresight."*

aftersight and foresight
the sound is dull
    in the ear
    like a bruise
    on fruit or
    taint
    in strong
    meat
So curious a man
    this Eliot
exquisite, pertinent,
yet dimmed in his climax

aftersight and foresight
    hole upon hole
    a curse
    upon prosody
    even when T.S.
    sponsors
    the hole.

I have a simple mind
  and write my words
  to sweep across
  a broad cloth.
Rich talents go often
  to misers who make
  diadems of chocolate.
    *the emperor is*
    *the emperor of ice cream*

Yes, the rich speak only
  to the purls of their lace.
  I want the whole wipe
  of the cloth

Or do I delude myself
  and merely spit like
  a hoodlum
  into the wake of phaetons
  that drive away?

A writer who
has power
should use it
to extract
such benefits
from his
publisher

as
give
his
words

room
to
breathe

I want my line to strike like a snake

A snake
can't strike
in a box

you break
up your
line
like
ee
cum
mings
I notice

n
o heb re a
ksitu pd
iffe
r
e
nt

I am looking
for the
fish who
swim in the
spaces

ee likes the
herbs
in the
letters

r)
ette

besi desh e'sb

Falling in love has
left my work in a mess.

I have no desire
to change. My
spirit is to be
critical.

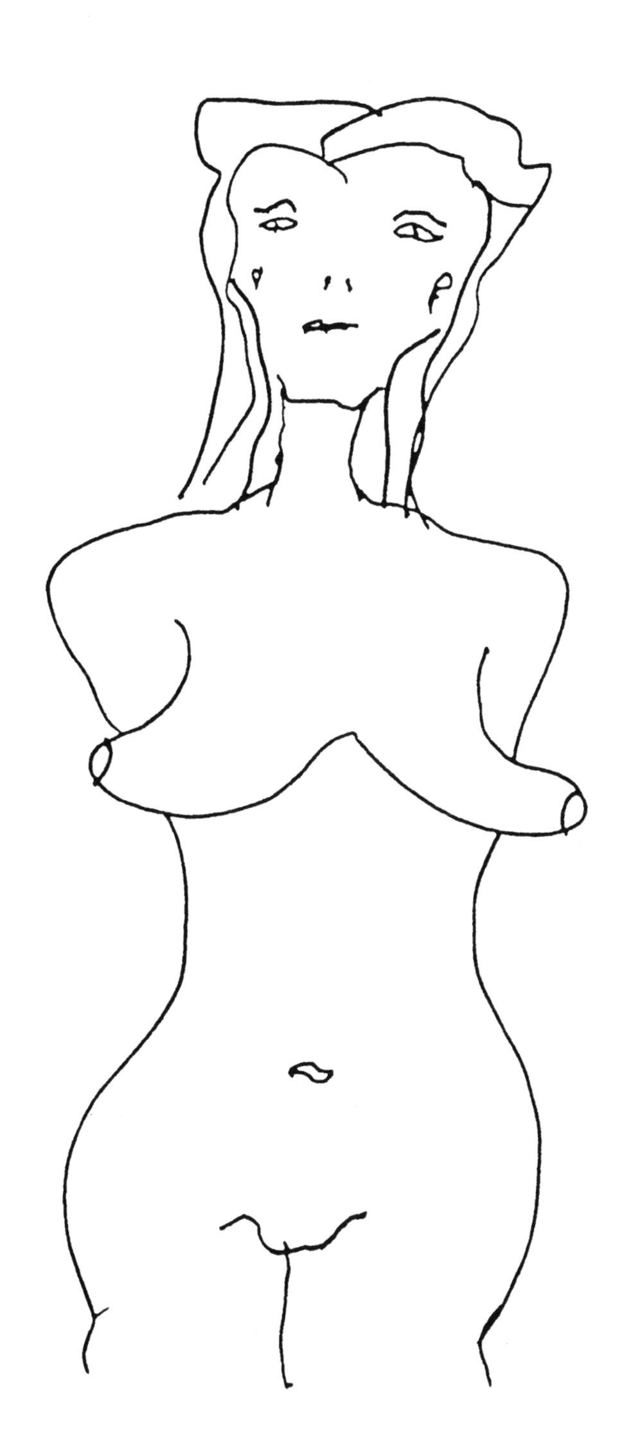

I'm very
critical
until I
take off
my clothes.

Some poems
are mild
and pleasant
little children
who bear no title
and need none
one doesn't notice
their
nakedness

A title
is not
a hat
but
a suit
so
sometimes
I leave
it at the
bottom of
the page,
for
I don't want
all these poems
to be
unclothed.
Some should be
standing
with
their trousers
dropped to
their shoes.
Of course
by this logic
a title at the head
is like a dress
lifted over the breast

Poems
written by
masochists
flop like cows
in the meadow.
Take pity on me
they cry, pay
attention, I
am so sensitive
to nature and
full of milk

Poems
should be like pins
that prick the skin
of boredom
and leave
a glow
equal in its pride
to the gait
of the sadist
who stuck
the pin
and walked away

# Justice

She's a
bitch
said
the witch
in a tone
that clarified
the eternal meaning
of the consonants.

No, your honor,
said my voice.
Without vowels
there is no
justice
in human verdict.

We were speaking
of bitches
said
the judge
Ignore eternity
and the color
she gives to legal
utterance
It is better
to chase consonants
than vowels.
consonants are
fact and force
clear as compound
interest

vowels are hot eyes
in hard bodies
bleeding for trouble.

But I replied:
Eternity is first heard
on the pigeon's wing
of a sigh
breathing alas at
all that passes
and does not live
Judge, Your Honor,
Bind me over
to the next of size
for I do dream
that love there may be
in human flow.

## Danger

Words in the nerve
of becoming
are feathers
    of eternity
    (insofar
        as a poem may become
        the death of another
        who believed the poem
        and so ended in some alley
        of bad venture
        with the wrong foe)

those
who are alive
look to others
for a mirror
half dead, one drinks
alone at night
and writes poems
bad ones said self
sorry pity
should write so sad
and beg for tears

I've
learned
to live
with the
divisions
in my
soul.

## The Corners of a Square

1.

It would
be
an aid
if the
blind
came
to the
game
because
their ears
are
clean
said
the dream.

2.

I would
be
afraid
of those
who
hear and
do not
see
said
the word.

3.

I am
in
love with
those who
come
with their
wound to
me
said the
mood
for
those who
see
and do
not hear
wound
others
with their
voice

4.

Those who
hear
and do
not see
give
alms
to Eve
and
other
ill
said
the peace
that comes
from
the police.

Let
at least
a drink
be
named
after me
said the poet
sealing his
fate
for
no bar
in the land
would tease
the police.

# XIV

# Politicians

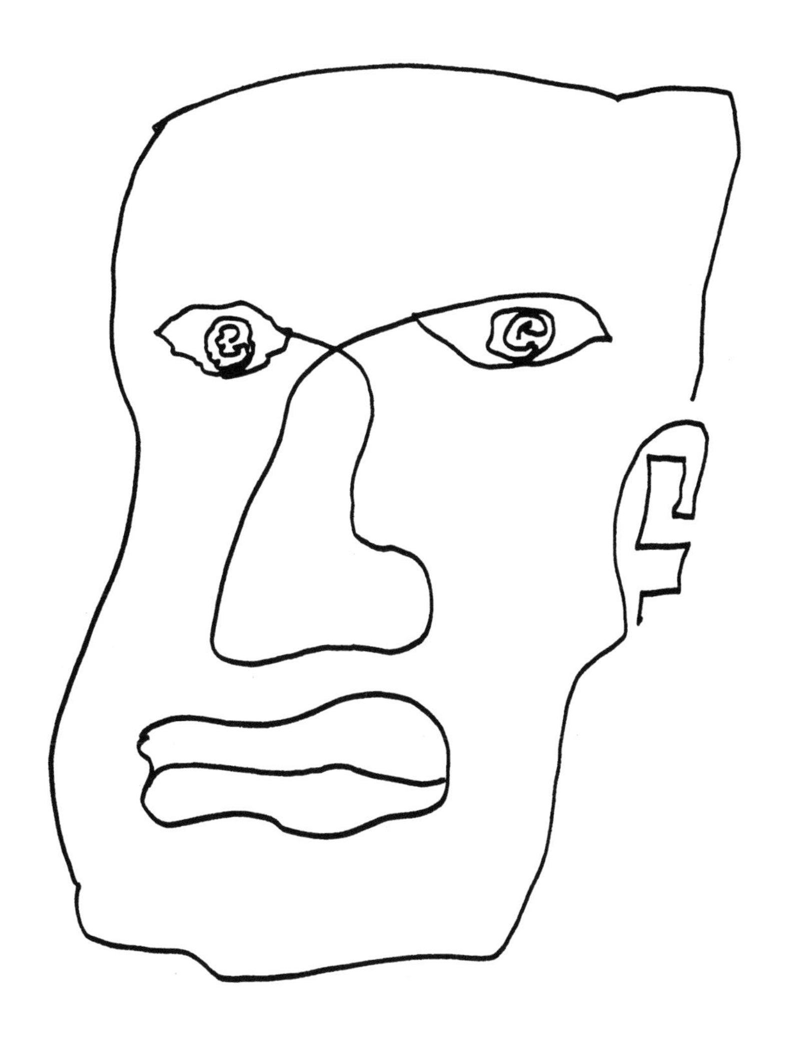

We're looking to mine
the bottom line.
Down where the Undecided
hang out.

I see no reason to put
my trust in any politician

It was easy. I never spent time with a man who was of no use to me.

OLD
BATTERED
BILLY-BOY
CLINTON

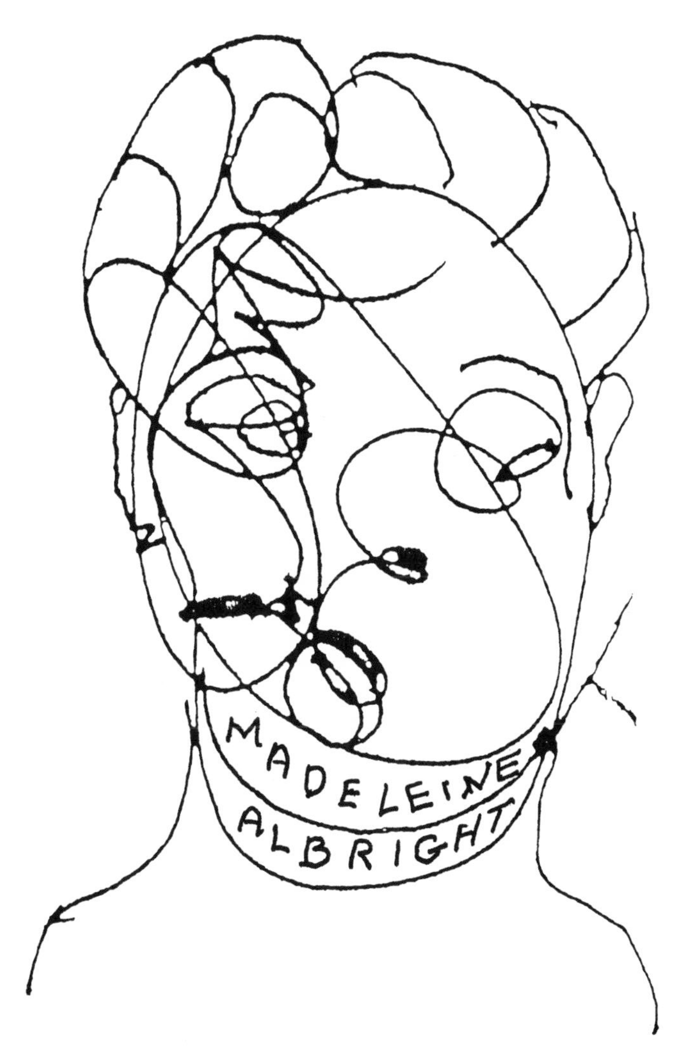

My knowledge of foreign affairs is immaculate. Kosovo! Kosovo!

People keep asking me if I'm Ariel Sharon

People keep telling me
that I look like George W.
but I opt for Superman.

## Exodus

Goodbye America
Jesus said.
Come back, boy!
We cried too late.

# XV

# Hemingway Revisited

Jake pissed
with
stern
loneliness
leaving
a fierce
smell
of the past.
His future
was not
so empty
as he declared,
a girl with
music and grace
tender of face
was waiting
for him.

Hey—
you
sleep
deep—
but what a sight
see
you
soon
beautiful
I hope

Catherine
found this note
by her telephone
on awakening
in an empty bed
after a one night
stand and she called
her best friend
to say;
Guess what?
I feel like
Earth
Mother.

Catherine never blushed
until
she smelled
the fine cheat
in
the line
of the succession
and then
she flushed
furiously
for she thought
the smell
adorable,
it was
so
rich
to rise
from
the poor.

We really ought, Catherine said
to be able to stay together
without making love
all the time.

Yes, said Jake,
I'm sure it's my fault.

Yes, she said smugly
you smell so greedy
                    and good

Swarms and swarms
  of love
  smug, smug, smug.

You may not love me<br>
                    Jake said<br>
          but I love you.<br>
Well, I love you,<br>
          said Catherine<br>
          so<br>
          bad luck.<br>
They loved each other<br>
          very much.<br>
They had not taken<br>
          a good wash<br>
          in three weeks.<br>
It would have been<br>
          the next wrong<br>
          to murdering<br>
              a child.<br>
What the hell<br>
          they were both<br>
          thirty<br>
          forty<br>
          tired, tried,<br>
          sad, foul<br>
They thought they<br>
          had betrayed<br>
          something<br>
          forever,<br>
And She forgave them.<br>
Or thus they hoped.<br>
          So, bad luck<br>
          muttered the<br>
               horror<br>
               of old<br>
               habit,<br>
               We will die<br>
               if we lose<br>
               our love.

Mangled, morgued
birched and bruted
they were
hawks
upon the mood
of their
own blessing.

So they scattered,
waiting
for the
curse.

Slack the yaws
tight the jaws
hurricane
the air
of waiting

Will you play "The Lady is a Tramp?"

I feel
like
I've been
through purga-
tory, Catherine
said.

Sometimes
I think
it won't
be bad
when
we die
because
we've served
part
of
purgatory al-
ready.

Oh, darling, good, she agreed,
so good.
I used to think
it would
be always,
but it wasn't, it
turned out
to be
such a little
taste
of
heaven
for twelve
long years.

Yes.
It's been
bad.
But
twelve years
ago
we were
good.

A little taste
of heaven
is all we get, baby,
said Jake.
through the
microphone
and plate
glass
window
of the visitor's
room
under
the shotguns
eyes
bellies
and blue serge suits
of the guards
who guard
the sacred heart
of the Republic.

# XVI

# The Harbors of The Moon

I used
to think
my life
would be
a
destiny
and now
I realize
it's but a fate
said a man
I met
in Bellevue
for
stabbing
his
brother
with a
kitchen
knife.

One
nerve
screams
before
you
fall
said
the
ledge
on
the
window
of
the
nineteenth
floor

## Death of a Lover Who Loved Death

1.

I find
that
most
of the people I
know
are immature
and cannot
cope
with reality
said the suicide.
His death
followed
a slash on each wrist.

He coped with
reality
well.

2.

It was unreality
which waited
on a midnight trail
in that
jungle of eternity
he heard murmuring
on the other side.

Oh, night of the jungle,
God of mercy
wept the suicide
do not ask me
to reconnoiter
this
dark
trail
when I am now
without
hands.

## In the Jardin Exotique of Eze

In the Jardin Exotique of Eze
the cactus come up from the sea
like an anemone wooing a spider
or a pygmy with a blowgun dart.
Silently they smell the breeze,
          invertebrate,
their memory as long as the tripe of the Mediterranée.
Was it once or never? that a God from deep waters
                    dreaming of the moon
fell in love with a gleam from the midnight sky
who, intoxicated with herself
and the rapture of the depths,
like a daughter most fortunate in family,
beautiful, spoiled, innocent of alarm,
wandered down an alley
dark as the pitch of blackest frustration
and there was trapped by the sound of need
in the murmur of an ape.
So did the God of dark waters woo a moon beam
and from their love leave a seed
on the spume of the wrack
which washes a desert shore
Cactus,
mad psychotic bulb of light and dark
          spy of the deep sea
          intimate of the moon

your form inspires nausea
for love that dares too much
and has no soil but sand
flowers spines of lunar hatred
shapes tubers on the leaf
and gives no wine but visions from peyote
of ether and her gardens
which burn with the
death of suns
and phosphorescent nights.

## The Executioner's Song

I think if I had three good years to give
  in study at some occupation
  that was fierce and new
  and full of stimulation
I think I would become
            an executioner
  with time spent out in the field
  digging graves for bodies I had made
              the night before.
You see: I am bad at endings
my bowels move without honor
  and flatulence is an affliction
  my pride must welcome with gloom
It comes I know from preoccupation
  much too much with sex
Those who end well do not spend their time
  so badly on the throne

For this reason I expect the task
  of gravedigger welcomes me
I would like to kill well and bury well
Perhaps then my seed would not shoot
  so frantic a flare.
If I could execute neatly
  (with respect for whatever romantic
                                   imagination
gave passion to my subject's crime)

and if I buried well
(with tenderness, dispatch, gravity
and joy that the job was not jangled—
giving a last just touch of the spade
to the coffin
                    in order to leave it
quivering
              like a leaf—for forget not
coffins quiver as the breath goes out
and the earth comes down)

Yes,
if I could kill cleanly
and learn not to turn my back
on the face of each victim
as he chooses
                    what is last to be seen
in his eye,
               well, then perhaps,
then might I rise so high upon occasion
as to smite a fist of the Lord's creation
into the womb of that muse
which gives us poems
Yes, then I might
For one ends best when death is clean
   to the mind
                      and calm in its proportion
fire in the orchard and flame at the root.

All the men I've killed weigh
upon my soul until I no longer
know whether I am a Russian
or a Chechen.

Is mood a temple
 to give us
 sanctuary
 against
  the desire
  of our cells
  to return to
   their beginnings
   under a
   new master
   who promises
   that he
   will not
   repeat
  the hesitations,
  compassions
    and
  aesthetic
    com-
  punctions of God
   about
    pleasure
    profit
   and
    progress
   but
    instead
     will rip up
     the roots
and give us
the broad
macadam
  of
eternity without fire

and sucaryl
for the syrup
     of the peach.

## A Wandering in Prose: for Hemingway, Summer 1956

Why do you still put on that face
powder which smells like Paris when
I was kicking Seconal and used to
get up at four in the morning and
walk the streets into the long wait
for dawn (like an exhausted husband
pacing the room where you wait for
the hospital to inform you of wife
and birth) visions of my death
already in the nauseas off my tense
frightened liver—such a poor death,
wet with timidity, ordure and the
muck of a Paris dawn, the city more
beautiful than it had ever been, warm
in June and me at five in an Algerian
bar watching the workers take a
swallow of wine for breakfast, the
city gentle in its light even to me
and I sicker than I've ever been,
weak with loathing at all I had not done,
and all I was learning of all I would
now never do, and I would come back
after combing the vistas of the Seine
for glints of light to bank in the
corroded vaults of my ambitious and
yellow jaundiced soul and there back

in bed, nada, you lying in bed in hate
of me, the waves of unspoken flesh
radiating detestation into me because
I have been brave a little but not nearly
brave enough for you, greedy bitch,
Spanish lady, with your murderous
Indian blood and your crazy purity
hung on courage in men as if it were
your queen's own royal balls, and I
would lie down next to you, that smell
of unguent and face powder bleak and
chic as if the life of your skin depended
now not on the life my hands could give
in a pass upon your cheek, but upon the
arts of the corporation mixing your
elixirs in hundred gallon vats by
temperatures calibrated to the thermostat,
bleak and chic like the Hotel Palais
Royale ("my home away from home" we had
seen written by Capote in his cuneiform
script when the guest book was passed
to me for the equivocal cachet of my
signature so dim in its fashion that
year) and I took up the pen thinking
of the buff-colored damp of our indif-
ferent room where we slept in misery
wondering if we had lost the loots of
anticipation we had commanded once so
fierce in one-another—or was it only
me? for that is the thought of a lover
when his death comes over him in that

scent of the creams you rubbed on your
face while I slept the half-sleep of
the addict kicking the authority of
his poison—how bitter and clean was
the taste of the Seconal. And now the scent
of that cream came over me again as you kissed
me here at this instant, wearing it
again, knowing I detest it because again
it drives the secret of my poor augure
for eternity into those caverns of my
nose which lead back among the stalactites
of the nostril to the dream and one's
nightly dialogue with the fine verdicts
of the city asleep, and all souls on the
prowl talking to one another in the
dark markets of heaven about the future
of what we are to be if one obeys the
shape we gamblers have given to that
tool of destiny—our character. And the
smell of the corporation is still on
your skin mocking what I have done to
mine.

## The Harbors of the Moon

I
know
a town
with
sighs
of
sea
smiled
the
white
witch

I know
a town
that
sails
the
sun

I know
a town
where
light
is dry
and
boats
come
home
with
silver
in their
hold

where
boats
come
home
with
silver
in their
hold

(do not
grieve
the
death
of
little
fish
They
are
lights
that
seek
the
deep)

I know
a town
with
sighs
of sea

white
with
the
tides
of me

white
as the
spine
of the
sea.

finis

APPENDIX

# Introduction to *Deaths for the Ladies (and other disasters)*

*Deaths for the Ladies* was written through a period of fifteen months, a time when my life was going through many changes, including a short stretch in the prison ward of Bellevue, the abrupt dissolution of one marriage, and the beginning of another. It was also a period in which I wrote very little, and so these poems and short turns of prose were my lonely connection to the one act that gave a sense of self-importance. I was drinking heavily in this period, not explosively as I had at times in the past but steadily—most nights, I went to bed with all the vats loaded, and for the first time my hangovers in the morning were steeped in dread. Before, I had never felt weak without a drink—now I did. I felt heavy, hard on the first steps of middle age, and in need of a drink. So it occurred to me it was finally not altogether impossible that I become an alcoholic. I hated the thought of that. My pride and my idea of myself were subject to slaughter in such a vice.

Well, this preface is not to recount the story of those years and how I may have come out of them; no, we are here to give a crack of light to the little book that follows. I used to wake up in those days, as I have just remarked, with a drear hangover, and the beasts who were ready to root in my entrails were prowling outside. To a man

living on his edge, New York is a jungle, and such mornings were full of taboo. It was often directly important whether the right or left hand was crossed with water first.

One modest reality used to save such hours from dipping too quickly into too early a drink. It was the scraps of paper I would find in my jacket. There were fragments of poems on the scraps, not poems really, little groupings of lines, little crossed communications from some wistful outpost of my mind where, deep in drink the night before, it had seemed condign to record the unrecoverable nuance of a moment, a funny moment, a mean moment, a moment when something I might always have taken for granted was turned for an instant on its head.

Some of those curious little communications that came riding in on the night through an electrolyte of deep booze were fairly good, many were silly, the best were often indecipherable. This would feel close to tragic. Almost always the sensation of writing a good poem (in the dark of early morning) was followed in the daylight by the knowledge I had gone so deep I could not find my eyes. My handwriting had temporarily disintegrated in the passion of putting down a few words. Somebody had obviously been awash in the rapture of the depths.

It was not so very funny. In the absence of a greater faith, a professional keeps himself in shape by remaining true to his professionalism. Amateurs write when they are drunk. For a serious writer to do that is equivalent to a professional football player throwing imaginary passes in traffic when he is bombed, and smashing his body into parked cars on the mistaken impression that he is taking out the linebacker. Such a professional football player will feel like crying in the morning when he discovers his ribs are broken.

I would feel like crying too. My pride, my substance, my capital, was to be found in my clarity of mind or—since my mind is never so very clear—let us say found in the professional cool with which the brain was able to contend with the temptations and opportunities each leap of intuition offered. It was criminal to take these leaps like an amateur, steeped in drink, wasteful, wanton. To be hearing the inspirations of the angel when one is kissing the fumes is a condition so implicit with agony that it took eighteen centuries of Christendom before Kierkegaard could come back alive with the knowledge that such moments not only existed but indeed were the characteristic way modern man found a knowledge of his soul—which is to say he found it by the act of perceiving that he was most certainly losing it.

I would go to work, however, on my scraps of paper. They were all I had for work. I would rewrite them carefully, printing in longhand and ink, and I would spend hours whenever there was time going over these little poems, these sharp dry crisp little instants, some of them no more and hopefully no less possessed of meaning than the little crack or clatter of an autumn leaf underfoot. Something of the wistfulness in the fall of the wind was in those poems for me. And since I wasn't doing anything else very well in those days, I worked the poems over every chance I had. Sometimes a working day would go by, and I would put a space between two lines or remove a word. Maybe I was mending. As the sense of work grew a little clearer and the hangover receded, there was a happiness working mornings on *Deaths for the Ladies* that I had not felt for years. I loved *Deaths for the Ladies,* not because it was a big book—I knew my gifts as a poet were determined to be small—but because I was in love with its modesty. The modesty of *Deaths for the Ladies* was saving me. Out of the bonfire I seemed to have

made of my life, these few embers were to be saved and set—not every last part of one's memories would have to be consumed. Besides, I wanted to give pleasure. It seemed to me that *Deaths for the Ladies* would give more simple pleasure than any book I had ever written, it was pure, it was modest, it was sad, and it was funny—it was so very modest—how could one not like it? And it even had one innovation to offer poets—so I thought. There was no music or prosody or command or rush of language in the book, no power, not much meter, not at all, much of it was poetry only by the arbitrary insistence of the short line, but *Deaths for the Ladies* was something else, I thought—it was a movie in words. I set it with the greatest care. Every line was placed on the page by me. The spaces were chosen with much deliberation, the repetitions of phrases were like images in a film. The music of the poem as a whole—if it had any—was like the montage of a film. I felt that all of *Deaths for the Ladies* made up one poem, not all that great a poem, never in any way, but still a modest poem about a man loose in our city, for one cannot talk of New York without saying our city, there, majestic, choking in its own passions, New York, the true capital of the Twentieth Century. And *Deaths for the Ladies* was like a small sea breeze running through some of those electronic canyons where a myriad of fine moments were forever dying in the iridescence of foam.

Of course, if you fall in love with a book, you may be certain it will drown, suffocate, or expire all alone on an untended bed. *Deaths for the Ladies* came out in modest edition and sank without a sound. It was only reviewed in three or four places, and the one good review it received (the Sunday *New York Times*) was six months late. Poets, for the most part, resented it. Why should they not? I had dabbled in that life for which

they were willing, if they were good enough, to starve and lose love. They had studied their craft; I had just skipped about in it. They were dedicated to poetry, I was dedicated to climbing out of the hole I had dug for myself, and poetry was offering the first rung. Therefore poets ignored the book, which was a pity, for a good poet might have done something with my little innovation, my movie in words.

But to end on a note less altruistic to the interests of art, let us look at one review. I had secret hopes, I now confess, that *Deaths for the Ladies* would be a vast success at the bar of poetry. The hopes got bounced. Here is the review in *Time,* March 30, 1962:

Ever<br>
see<br>
a drunk<br>
come on<br>
daring<br>
I mean<br>
drunk<br>
like<br>
daring<br>
was a<br>
sloppy<br>
entrechat?<br>
Mr M<br>
comes on<br>
with fourbucks<br>
of poems<br>
about sex<br>
not love<br>
that run<br>
down<br>
like this<br>
only<br>
not<br>
lined up<br>
neat.<br>
Having less

than
fourbucks
fun
a reader
counted
the words
and concluded
Mr M
is making up
for his
first book
which had
too many.
You didn't
score
this
time
M
a
n

But hell you know that.

In a fury of incalculable pains, a poem was written in reply, sent to *Time* magazine's column of letters, and printed there.

Poem to the Book Review at *Time*

You will keep hiring
        picadors from the back row
        and pic the bull back
        far back along his spine
You will pass wine
        poisoned on the vine
You will saw the horns off
        and murmur
The bulls are
        ah, the bulls are not
        what once they were

Before the corrida is over
        there will be Russians in the plaza
Swine some of you will say
what did we wrong?
And go forth to kiss the conquerer.

Now, on the comfortable flank of this reminiscence, I think I may have been fortunate to get so paltry a reception on *Deaths for the Ladies.* For if I had been treated well, I might have kept floating on a still little pond and drowned my sorrow for myself in endless wine and scraps of paper and folios of further poems. Instead, the review in *Time* put iron into my heart again, and rage, and the feeling that the enemy was more alive than ever, and dirtier in the alley, and so one had to mend, and put on the armor, and go to war, go out to war again, and try to hew huge strokes with the only broadsword God ever gave any good writer—a glimpse of something like Almighty prose.

# Acknowledgments

I would like to thank David Ebershoff, Dwayne R. Prickett,
Danielle Mailer, J. Michael Lennon,
and Judith McNally for their
careful reading and criticism
of this book.

## ABOUT THE AUTHOR

NORMAN MAILER was born in 1923 and published his first book, *The Naked and the Dead,* in 1948. *The Armies of the Night* won the National Book Award and the Pulitzer Prize in 1969; Mailer received another Pulitzer in 1980 for *The Executioner's Song.* His most recent books, both published by Random House, are *The Spooky Art* and *Why Are We at War?* He lives in Provincetown with his wife, Norris Church Mailer.

ALSO BY NORMAN MAILER

*The Naked and the Dead*
*Barbary Shore*
*The Deer Park*
*Advertisements for Myself*
*Deaths for the Ladies (and other disasters)*
*The Presidential Papers*
*An American Dream*
*Cannibals and Christians*
*Why Are We in Vietnam?*
*The Deer Park—A Play*
*The Armies of the Night*
*Miami and the Siege of Chicago*
*Of a Fire on the Moon*
*The Prisoner of Sex*
*Maidstone*
*Existential Errands*
*St. George the Godfather*
*Marilyn*
*The Faith of Graffiti*
*The Fight*
*Genius and Lust*
*The Executioner's Song*
*Of Women and Their Elegance*
*Pieces and Pontifications*
*Ancient Evenings*
*Though Guys Don't Dance*
*Harlot's Ghost*
*Oswald's Tale: An American Mystery*
*Portrait of Picasso as a Young Man*
*The Gospel According to the Son*
*The Time of Our Time*
*The Spooky Art*
*Why Are We at War?*

# Contents

## B. Lingerers, Laggards & Blackguards

## II. Maladies of Centralists

## III. Levels of Procurement

## IV. The Mediocre

## V. A One Night Stand

## VI. Unhappy Marriage

## VII. A Drunken Marriage

## VIII. Drinking to Eternity

## IX. Intermission
(During the Intermission There Will Be a Variety Show)

## X.
### A. Interplanetary Is Trans-temporal

### B. In Which We Visit the Abductionally Challenged

## XI. The Upper Classes
### A. Transatlantic

### B. Witches and Warlocks

## C. Camembert and Caviar

## XII. The Lower Classes

## XIII. Hunting for Poems

## XIV. Politicians

## XV. Hemingway Revisited

## XVI. The Harbors of the Moon

A Random House Trade Paperback Original

 Published in the United States by Random House Trade Paperbacks, an imprint of The Random House Publishing Group, a division of Random House, Inc., New York, and simultaneously in Canada by Random House of Canada Limited, Toronto.

Random House Trade Paperbacks and colophon are trademarks of Random House, Inc.

The poems in this work were originally published in *Cannibals and Christians* (New York: The Dial Press, 1966), copyright © 1965 by Norman Mailer, and in *Deaths for the Ladies (and other disasters)* (New York: G. P. Putnam's Sons, 1962), copyright © 1962 by Norman Mailer.

Grateful acknowledgment is made to *Time* magazine for permission to reprint excerpts from "Review of 'Deaths for the Ladies' " from *Time* magazine, March 30, 1962, copyright © 1962 by Time, Inc. Reprinted by permission.

Library of Congress Cataloguing-in-Publication Data
Mailer, Norman.
Modest gifts : poems and drawings / by Norman Mailer.
p. cm.
ISBN 0-8129-7237-6
I. Title.
PS3525.A4152A6 2003
811'.54—dc22 2003058552

Random House website address: www.atrandom.com

Printed in the United States of America

2 4 6 8 9 7 5 3 1